ISLAM, ECONOMICS, AND SOCIETY

ISLAM, ECONOMICS, AND SOCIETY

Syed Nawab Haider Naqvi

KEGAN PAUL INTERNATIONAL
London and New York

First published in 1994 by
Kegan Paul International Ltd
UK: P.O. Box 256, London WC1B 3SW, England
USA: 29 West 35th Street, New York, NY 10001-2299, USA

Distributed by
John Wiley & Sons Ltd
Southern Cross Trading Estate
1 Oldlands Way, Bognor Regis
West Sussex PO22 9SA, England

Routledge, Inc
29 West 35th Street
New York, NY 10001-2299, USA

© Syed Nawab Haider Naqvi, 1994

Phototypeset in Palatino 10 on 12 pt
by Intype, London
Printed in Great Britain by TJ Press Ltd, Padstow, Cornwall

All rights reserved. No part of this book may be reprinted
or reproduced or utilized in any form or by any electronic,
mechanical or other means, now known or hereafter invented,
including photocopying and recording, or in any information
storage or retrieval system, without permission in writing
from the publishers.

British Library Cataloguing in Publication Data
Naqvi, Syed Nawab Haider
Islam, Economics, and Society
I. Title
297.19785

ISBN 0-7103-0470-6

Library of Congress Cataloging-in-Publication Data
Naqvi, Syed Nawab Haider.
  Islam, economics, and society / Syed Nawab Haider Naqvi.
    180pp. 22cm.
    Includes bibliographical references (p.164) and index.
  ISBN 0-7103-0470-6
    1. Economics—Religious aspects—Islam. 2. Islam—Economic
  aspects. I. Title.
  BP173.75.N3734 1993
  330. 1—dc20   93-2443
                                                              CIP

Dedicated
to
my wife Saeeda
and our daughters
Andalib, Tehmina, Qurratulain
and Neelofar

بسم الله الرحمن الرحيم

IN THE NAME OF ALLAH,
THE MERCIFUL,
THE MERCY-GIVING

CONTENTS

Foreword by Professor Khurshid Ahmad ... xi
Preface ... xvii

Chapter 1   Introduction ... 1
   Plan of Work ... 5

PART I: FOUNDATIONAL ISSUES

Chapter 2   The Nature and Significance of Islamic Economics ... 13
   A Matter of Definition ... 13
   Ethics and Economics ... 15
      The Belief in the Divine Presence ... 15
      Muslim Society versus the Islamic Society ... 16
   On Assessing Islamic Economics ... 17
   Does Islamic Economics Exist? ... 18
   Summary ... 20

Chapter 3   The Ethical Foundations ... 24
   An Outline of Islamic Ethics ... 24
   The Ethical Axioms ... 26
      Unity (*Tawhid*) ... 26
      Equilibrium (*Al Adl wal Ihsan*) ... 27
      Free Will (*Ikhtiy'ar*) ... 29
      Responsibility (*Fardh*) ... 31
   Summary ... 34

CONTENTS

PART II: A MODEL OF ISLAMIC ETHICAL AXIOMS

Chapter 4　The Framing of Axioms of Islamic Ethics　41
　Religion as a Source of Ethical Axioms　41
　The Characteristics of the System of Ethical Axioms　42
　The 'Efficiency' of the Islamic Ethical Axiom System　44
　Towards a Normative Islamic Economics　47
　Summary　50

Chapter 5　The Rules of Economic Behaviour in an Islamic Economy　53
　From Axioms to Rules of Economic Behaviour　53
　Rational Behaviour and Ethical Environment　55
　　Ethics and Rational Behaviour　55
　　The 'Priority' of Individual Liberty　56
　　Ethics and Consumer Behaviour　57
　　Pareto-Optimality as a Social-Choice Rule?　60
　Ethics and Distributive Justice　61
　　Reducing Income Inequality　62
　　Structural Change　62
　Ethics and the Role of the Government　64
　The Problem of Social Choice in an Islamic Economy　66
　Summary　67

Chapter 6　A Perspective on Inter-Systemic Comparisons　71
　Islam and Socialism　72
　Islam and Capitalism　75
　Islam and the Welfare-State Doctrine　79
　Summary　80

PART III: THE OBJECTIVES AND POLICIES IN AN ISLAMIC ECONOMY

Chapter 7　Setting the Policy Objectives　87
　The Basic Objectives　88
　　Individual Freedom　88
　　Distributive Justice　89
　　Universal Education　91
　　Economic Growth　92

CONTENTS

Maximizing Employment Generation   94
Summary   95

Chapter 8   A Taxonomy of Policy Instruments   99
Some Key Policy Issues   100
    The Institution of Private Property   100
    Growth-Promoting Policies   103
    Social Security System   104
    The Question of Public Ownership   105
Summary   107

Chapter 9   The Problem of Abolishing Interest: I   110
A Few Clarifications   111
An Islamic Perspective on Interest   113
    The Problem of Positive Time Preference   114
    The Marginal Utility (Disutility) of Consumption (Savings) Over Time   115
    The Depreciation of Capital and New Investment   115
    Introducing Money   116
Summary   117

Chapter 10   The Problem of Abolishing Interest: II   120
Can Interest be Abolished by Administrative *Fiat*?   120
PLS, Equities, and Bonds   121
The Fixed Rate of Return vs The Variable Rate of Return   122
    From Interest Rates to Profit Shares   123
    The Preference for the Variable-Return Instruments   123
    Is Equity-Financing 'Separable' from Debt-Financing?   124
    Is Uncertainty *per se* Desirable?   125
The Ethic of the PLS   125
Summary   127

Chapter 11   Towards a Solution of the Problem of Interest   130
Regulating the PLS System   131
Indexing of the Rates of Return on Savings   132
    The Principle of Indexation   132
    Reforming Lending Operations   134
Summary   135

CONTENTS

PART IV: RAINBOW'S END

Chapter 12   From the Ideal to the 'Reality'   139
- The Challenge of Transition   139
- Financial Reforms in Pakistan   141
- The Pangs of Transition   144
- The 'Initial Conditions'   145
  - Private Property   146
  - Voluntary Combinations   147
  - Universal Education   148
- Summary   149

Chapter 13   Towards a New Social Reality   153
- A Leitmotif   154
- The Mainsprings of Islamic Economic Philosophy   156
- The Consequence-Sensitivity of the Islamic Economic Philosophy   158
- Why an Islamic Economy?   159
- The Force of Islamic Morality   160
- The Road to Success   161

References   164

Index   172

FOREWORD

While the mainstream economic paradigm remains entrenched in the corridors of learning and research, the real-world situation is persuading an increasing number of economists and economic policy-makers seriously to doubt the 'universality', 'realism', 'productivity', and even 'morality' of some of the basic assumptions and core concepts of this paradigm. Thomas Ulen captures the mood of a sizeable number of the community of economists when he says: 'many of the most recent presidential addresses to the American Economic Association have been highly critical of received micro- and macro-economic theory. However, there has not yet been an offering of a new paradigm' (Thomas S. Ulen, Review of Nelson and Winker's, *An Evolutionary Theory of Economic Change* in *Business History Review*, 1983, vol. 37, no. 4). Dissent and disagreement are no longer confined to the periphery; they are making serious dents on the centre core. What is being re-examined does not relate merely to policy perceptions and end-products; in fact the very assumptions about human nature, motivation, effort, and enterprise on which mainstream economics is based and the institutional framework in which the economic agent is expected to operate are placed under the spotlight. The current debate cannot be described as a search for new methodologies, formulations and prescriptions *within* the paradigm; it represents a serious effort to *search for a new paradigm* (Lester C. Thurrow, *Dangerous Currents*, Random House, New York, 1983; Amitai Etzioni, *The Moral Dimension: Towards a New Economics*, Macmillan, New York, 1988).

This is a very challenging moment in the history of the evolution of economics. Peter Drucker surmises: 'Reality has outgrown existing theories. This has happened twice before. The first occasion was in the years of the "divide" of the 1870s. Then the neo-classicists, Karl Menger in Austria, Stanley Jevons in England, and Leon Walras in France, created modern economics with their "marginal utility" theory. Then sixty years later, when the Great Depression confounded neo-classical theory, John Maynard Keynes created a new synthesis, the economic theory of the nation-state, in which the neo-classicists' marginal utility theory is a "sub-set", a "building block" rechristened as "microeconomics". Since then there have been only minor adjustments. Milton Friedman and the "supply siders" are "post-Keynesian" rather than "anti-Keynesian" ' (Peter F. Drucker, *The New Realities*, Oxford, 1989, p. 149).

The challenges that remain unresponded to are legion: inflation along with unemployment, recession that fails to respond to traditional stimuli, growth without social justice, breakdown of social security systems, budgetary deficits that defy control, mounting debts, both domestic and international, ecological crisis, emergence of the supra-national state without supra-national mechanisms and agents for economic policy-making, development fiasco in a large number of Third World countries, and increasing constraints for the developed world to play an effective role in alleviating the misery of a large part of suffering humanity.

An economic theory encased within the assumptions of the classical and neo-classical paradigm looks askance at this situation. The issues and challenges that confront the economist today are more complex, even more fundamental, than the ones faced by his predecessors. 'Challenged', writes Amitai Etzioni, 'is the entrenched utilitarian, rationalistic, individualistic, neo-classical paradigm which is applied not merely to the economy but also, increasingly to the full array of social relations, from crion to family' (*op. cit.*, p. ix). In fact, the economic paradigm is being challenged at its very core: the neo-classical paradigm does not merely ignore the moral dimensions but actively opposes its inclusion. The new paradigm, on the other hand, visualises assigning 'a key role for moral values'. Then alone may it be possible to 'seek both what is right *and* what is pleasurable' (ibid., p. ix, x).

It is in the context of this paradigmatic search that I consider the publication of Professor Syed Nawab Haider Naqvi's book *Islam, Economics, and Society* as significant. It may not only

FOREWORD

breathe some fresh air into the debate but also make a cogent contribution towards paving the way for the emergence of an alternative paradigm.

The real significance of the book lies in integrating ethics and economics into one consistent and interdependent framework – and in achieving this in such a realistic manner that the concern with the 'ordinary business of life' is neither diluted nor marginalised due to obsession with Utopia. I also look upon this work as a crucial bridge between the Western approach to economics and the literature produced by Muslim economists in their march towards Islamic economics.

Professor Naqvi has covered quite some mileage, ever since the publication of his earlier work *Ethics and Economies: An Islamic Synthesis* (1981). Although the approach remains familiar – reformulation of Islamic ethical values into a set of axioms, which could provide an essential as well as a sufficient framework for deducing behavioural norms as well as policy guidelines – yet his analysis here is more rigorous. Moreover the scope of the study has broadened to include an application to real-life situations in Muslim society. Some of his initial thoughts have been revised or modified while others have matured and been refined. The present volume is not only a treatise on Islamic economic philosophy, it also provides a framework for the reorganization of the economies of the Muslim countries. As such, it constitutes a stepping-stone towards the development of what could become a model of an Islamic economy.

Islamic economics is rooted in Islam's particular worldview and derives its value-premises for the ethico-social teachings of the Quran and *Sunnah*. This book makes the ethico-religious connections explicit; and the success, or lack of it, of an Islamic economy world be judged to the extent of its approximation to these values in the real-life situation.

Islam, Economics, and Society is also an important contribution towards a rigorous formulation of the nature and significance of Islamic economics. In his earlier work, *Ethics and Economics: An Islamic Synthesis,* Professor Naqvi successfully developed a systematic analytical framework containing most of the essential ethical values of Islam that could act as a basis for a logical deduction of the guidelines for economic policy. This axiological approach, starting with ethical philosophy via mathematical logic, led him to formulate major contours of an Islamic eco-

FOREWORD

nomic system. He demonstrated that this system is unique and is capable of simultaneously achieving growth and distributive justice, as well as guaranteeing individual freedom without sacrificing social well-being. In the present work, while consolidating and further refining his earlier contribution, Professor Naqvi has extended his methodology to study and explain the economic behaviour of a 'representative' Muslim in a typical, real-life Muslim society. This is a major step forward towards developing Islamic economics as a scientific discipline. The implications of this approach are challenging. It brings into sharp focus some of those dimensions which had remained hidden under the methodology of 'abstraction' and the assumption of 'universality' of economic behaviour. It shows what culture-bound economic behaviour is like; and unless this socio-cultural specificity is brought into the analytical framework, 'theory' would fail to explain 'reality' in its fullness. This also has challenging implications for the theorists and practitioners of Islamic economics. The whole practical dimension is brought under the scrutiny of analysis, which opens up a vast area for reflection, reconsideration, and research.

Professor Naqvi has shown pioneering vision in opening up this area by making a number of postulates of Islamic economics testable and verifiable. This is a promising area; but it has its problems and pitfalls. The contemporary Muslim world is still emerging from the long night of colonial hegemony: a period during which the key institutions of Muslim society were supplanted and substituted, the moral fibre of society was destroyed, and an 'unrepresentative' leadership was groomed to power, producing the most serious schism within Muslim society. The Muslim society of today is not yet a society on its own. It is still under the shadow of the Western system and, as such, it is doubtful how 'representative' of the Islamic ethos its current behaviour can be. That is why a note of caution must be added.

There is another normative dimension that could have been integrated into the present framework so assiduously developed by the author: the concept of the Ummah, its unity and solidarity; the normative aspect of co-operation, integration, and inter-dependence within the Ummah; and its self-reliance and its relationship with the rest.

Islamic economics is an evolving discipline. *Islam, Economics,*

FOREWORD

and Society by Professor Naqvi is destined to become a milestone on this evolutionary path like his earlier *Ethics and Economics: An Islamic Synthesis*. The tentative nature of many formulations at this stage is but natural. It would be unrealistic to expect otherwise. In my view, Professor Naqvi has made an original contribution to the debate about the key elements of Islamic economics. His unique contribution lies in bringing about greater systematization within Islamic economic thinking and in developing methodologies that have laid the foundation of a fruitful dialogue between Muslim economists and economists belonging to other traditions. I am sure *Islam, Economics, and Society* will further the debate among Muslim economists, as it will stimulate thinking among economists of the mainstream schools.

Khurshid Ahmad
Institute of Policy Studies
Islamabad, Pakistan
November 1993

PREFACE

The Islamic perception of the socio-economic process is dynamic and its insistence on social justice is uncompromising. This is because injustice disrupts social harmony and, for that very reason, is unethical. To produce the *best* social structure, according to this view, man's economic endeavours should be motivated by a meaningful moral philosophy.[1]

Thus, the Islamic view of economics is a sub-set of its cosmic ethical vision. It follows that to be able to make valid statements about the basic economic motivations and processes in the *Islamic* society – which is essentially an idealized version of a typical *Muslim* society – ethical propositions must be used as reference points. Such statements are essentially value judgements claiming objective validity, and they form the 'hard core' of Islamic economics, which seeks to describe a representative Muslim's economic behaviour in a *Muslim* society.

Seen against this perspective, the novelty of Islamic economics – as distinct from all other kinds of economics, i.e., the neoclassical economics, the Marxian economics, the institutional economics, etc. – lies in making its ethico-religious connections *explicit* at the very outset. However, it is one thing to assert that Islam ordains the reflection of ethical perceptions in man's economic motivations; but to assert that the former can be used as a basis for deriving the latter is a step further, and a difficult intellectual undertaking. It requires that Islamic ethics be transformed into a non-trivial, *irreducible* set of axioms (basic postulates), which are then used to deduce consistent rules of economic behaviour. One of the main goals of this book is to present an essentially ahistoric view of the Islamic ethical perception, in which a 'typical' Muslim *believes* without ques-

PREFACE

tion. Such a view is 'representable' by a set of four axioms, namely, Unity, Equilibrium, Free Will, and Responsibility. We claim that this set of axioms can be used to deduce logical statements of sufficient generality about Islamic economics; and that the statements so deduced are *falsifiable*, if not always *verifiable*, in the context of a real-life Muslim society.

The Islamic emphasis on Unity (*Tawhid*), which is the 'vertical' dimension of Islam, makes explicit the fact that the guidance (*hidayah*) with respect to the *right* course of action ultimately comes from God. It acts as a positive force for social integration for the simple reason that, in their servitude to God, all men are equal. They are also free, because no one has the right to enslave a fellow being; not even to barter away his *own* freedom for securing monetary or another kind of reward. Such a belief, held universally by Muslims, harnesses the voluntaristic urges of man for purposeful social action. Then, there is the 'horizontal' dimension of Islam, denoted by Equilibrium (al *'Adl wal Ihsan*), which requires creating a grand social balance. The adherence to Equilibrium denotes the 'straight path' of social harmony that avoids extremist behaviour.

Man's freedom to choose between alternative courses of action – including those between the polar extremes of good and evil – follows from his exalted position of being God's vicegerent (*Khalifa*) on earth, and his being entrusted with a Free Will. But to give man's God-given freedom a sense of direction and social purpose, it is anchored – through Responsibility – to an irrevocable commitment to the betterment of his fellow men. Essentially correlative to each other, Free Will and Responsibility seek to create a society where freedom is not only political and economic, but also the freedom from self-love, avarice, and greed – a freedom that springs from a strongly held longing to do good to others, *even* when it means making a sacrifice of one's own welfare.[2]

It follows that the Islamic view of economics differs from the viewpoints of other schools of thought – e.g., of capitalism, socialism, and welfare state – not just by an ethical factor, but also by its acceptance of *religion as the source of its ethic*. At a philosophical level, the inter-systemic differences arise from the fact that Islam insists on *changing* economic processes and institutions when these are *not* based on Equilibrium;[3] and holds that the motivation for such an 'activist' attitude derives from a representative Muslim's overall consciousness of God's Presence. The belief that one is being watched by God is accepted without question by Muslims. Thus, taking an ethical position in the pursuit of the day-to-day business of life is a 'reality' that must feature in any model of (Muslim) man, if only because of the 'intensity' with which such a position is normally taken.[4]

However, to assert the dominance of ethics over economics is not to say that economic conditions do not influence the ethical behaviour of human beings.[5] This assertion simply means that ethical considerations are both significant and decisive as guides of man's economic behaviour. Thus the Islamic view can be seen as contrary to the Marxian view, which relegates ethics to a lower level, though not ignoring it altogether, by insisting that it is the economic conditions prevailing in any society – i.e., the relations of production that become stabilized and reproduce themselves long enough to assume the status of 'structures' – that provide the mould to form its ethical perceptions. Islam does not subscribe to the Benthamite utilitarian philosophy either, according to which whatever maximizes the (unweighted) sum-total of individual happiness is socially good and right, *irrespective of how it is distributed*; nor would it accept the libertarian non-consequentialist moral rights philosophy, which prohibits 'patterning' of the exercise of private property rights. Instead, the individual's happiness is *redefined* in Islam to include both personal welfare and the welfare of others – especially of the poor and the deprived, who have a *prior* right on the wealth of the rich. Thus, no structure of property rights is beyond remedy if it is inconsistent with the dictates of social justice.

These considerations led me to write my earlier book, *Ethics and Economics: An Islamic Synthesis* (1981a). Ten years have passed since that book appeared.[6] In the interim, I have given some more thought to the discipline of Islamic economics, and to the challenges to which the new discipline must respond to be scientifically acceptable. It is now clear to me that Islamic economics does *not* explain economic behaviour in some utopian Islamic society, where all or most men have been 'reborn' according to the Islamic ethical principles. Instead, Islamic economics is about enunciating a significant number of falsifiable statements about the economic behaviour of 'representative' Muslims in a typical real-life *Muslim* society with reference to the ideals that impart it a distinct 'personality'.[7] Having understood this, the next conceptual hurdle to cross is to show that a representative Muslim's observable economic behaviour is different enough from that of the economic agents in other cultural-religious traditions to warrant a separate treatment; and that such differences in the behaviour pattern can be explained in terms of the pervasive acceptance of the Islamic ethic as an ideal form of behaviour in typical Muslim societies.

Such an analytical motivation is significant in many ways. First, it reflects the author's belief that economic doctrines are essentially an idealization of reality and *relative* to the nature of a society. They are not a collection of absolute, unchanging truths. Hence, such a body of knowledge must respond to large *exogenous* 'shocks', especially when they relate to a change in the societal context. If this was not so, it will no longer be possible to test economic theories – or, in Karl Popper's terminology, to *falsify* them. Second, it is my contention that ignoring modern Muslim societies while theorizing about Islamic economics will be a pointless exercise because theories, or models, simulate the real world, even though they do *not* describe it in every detail. Third, taking real-life Muslim societies into account also draws attention to the need for creating in them 'scientific communities' [Popper (1980)], which are distinguished by a critical attitude towards their discipline.

A direct result of the proposed analytical framework is that the present book is *not* an apologia, nor does it represent an attempt at reification. On the other hand, an effort has been made here to present the Islamic point of view about economic processes and to highlight its *distinctive* character in relation to other ideologies – namely, capitalism, socialism, and welfare state – in terms of its explicit insistence on a set of ethical principles significantly different from those held in other cultures. In other words, the emphasis in this book is on pointing out the reasons why an Islamic economic *system* – which at present remains a mere logical possibility rather than an actuality – will be preferred by the Muslims to other systems; it is *not* to prove the superiority of the Islamic system, in some absolute sense, over other systems. Such a proof can only be provided by Muslim societies in the real world – by showing that the system they believe in can be implemented and can better tackle specific economic issues. Thus, what is preferred in hypothetical situations may *not* be preferred in a real-world context if, because of a failure of design or implementation, an Islamic economic system does not succeed in meeting the economic challenges of modern times – of ensuring economic growth with distributive justice and keeping a balance between individual freedom and social responsibility.

As we reaffirm our faith in Islam as the source of all ethical beliefs held by Muslims in a typical Muslim society, and as we use these beliefs as reference points for making economic statements, it is essential to leave enough room for discussion and dissent instead of suppressing freedom of thought and expression in the name of religion. For Islam to become the source of a new intellectual paradigm, it should be freed from anachronistic ideas, traditions, and institutions – *even those created under the influence of the writings of the great Muslim jurists.* Islam must be understood to mean in practice what it professes to be – a religion emphasizing the equality of all mankind before God, and in relation to each other; a creed propagating tolerance towards differences in points of view, even those of a fundamental nature; a faith providing protection to the poor and the weak against the tyranny of the rich and the powerful while granting all the essential economic (and other) freedoms to man; and, above all, a way of life in which faith is neither inconsistent with reason nor hostile to a culture of scientific inquiry. With such an agenda for an Islamic research programme, Islam's economic teachings will have to be reinterpreted in the context of modern social thought. When this is done, there will be no place for those who employ religion as an instrument of personal ambition and kill the seeds of progressive thought even before they have struck roots.

Recognizing the fact that they are writing about Muslim societies, Muslim economists should not create the impression that they are enunciating some synthetic, universal truths.[8] Instead, they should be ready to subject their theories to the toughest tests, and to discard 'old' theories once enough contrary evidence, *a priori* and/or empirical, becomes available. The aim should be *scientific progress* in Islamic economics. From this point of view, great harm will be done to the growth of Islamic economics as a scientific discipline if all its 'statements' are treated with unnecessary respect and awe, and if its practitioners talk about their discipline only in reverential tones.

PREFACE

In undertaking the present work, I have been greatly helped by the writings of Seyyed Hossein Nasr, Syed Husain M. Jafri, Baqir Sadr,[9] Mahmud Taleghani, Frithjof Schuon, Syed Qutb, Muhammad Iqbal, Syed Ameer Ali, and Khurshid Ahmad. Some of the main ideas of this book have been spelled out in my earlier work, especially *Ethics and Economics: An Islamic Synthesis*, and in some of my subsequent writings on the subject. But in the present work, due to a radical change of analytical focus noted above, I have sought sharper results to yield additional insights into the characteristics of the Islamic economic system. In my view, the 'axiomatic' approach to Islamic economics remains an adequate analytical tool to work out, in terms of modern scientific knowledge, the basic elements of Islamic economics. This approach, if applied consistently, should help us to assimilate in our models of Islamic economics whatever in modern economics does not contradict the Islamic ethical axioms. By the same token, our method does not allow indiscriminate borrowing of ideas from the non-Islamic economic systems.

Thus, we reject the conservative view, which ignores all modern knowledge because, supposedly, Muslim scholars of several hundred years ago have already said everything useful. We also do not subscribe to the view that to differentiate our 'product' from Western economic thought, we should not make use of the latter's analytical tools; or that we should not use 'tainted' Western terminology even when it has been redefined in the Islamic context. It does not make sense to maintain that we must destroy all modern knowledge to be able to say anything genuinely new and Islamic. Fortunately, the proponents of such ideas do not occupy the mainstream of Islamic economics; and most of the practitioners of the new discipline accept the urgent need to undertake new research in the area without being overly rejectionist.

We also do not accept the view that there is no need for Islamic economics because the science of economics is adequate to analyse economic problems in all societies at all times. In particular, we reject the positivistic view that economics should remain untouched by ethics. Instead, we subscribe to an essentially broader view of economics which freely employs value judgements as scientific statements claiming objective validity; and take the additional step of recognizing religion as a source of ethics. To this end, as well as clarifying its holistic character, we have taken a multi-disciplinary route through mathematical logic, philosophy, and ethics to highlight the distinctive characteristics of Islamic economics. With respect to Western economics, we have been eclectic; and, paying due regard to the special features of Muslim society, we have also been relativistic. In doing so, our aim has been to *create* new knowledge, not just adapt what our forefathers wrote.

In exploring various issues in Islamic economics, I have held fruitful discussions with many of my close friends. I owe a lot to the encouragement and moral support of Mr Ghulam Ishaq Khan, formerly the President of the Islamic Republic of Pakistan. I am deeply indebted to Professor Khurshid Ahmad for his guidance and for contributing a foreword to this book. I am most grateful to Dr Gowher Rizvi for facilitating the publication of this book, and to Professor M. Ali Khan for reading through the entire manuscript and making many insightful comments. Special thanks are due to Dr Mohammad Afzal and Dr Sadi Cindoruk for their involvement in making the publication of this book possible. Thanks are also due to my old friends Mr H. U. Beg, Prof. Mian M. Nazeer, Prof. Rafiq Ahmed, Dr Asghar Qadir and to my former students and colleagues Drs Muhammad Anwar, Tayyeb Shabbir, Ather Maqsood Ahmed, Ashfaque H. Khan, Zafar Mahmood for their readiness to engage in useful discussion on many of the topics discussed in this book. The reviews of my earlier book, *Ethics and Economics: An Islamic Synthesis* – especially those by Syed Hossein Nasr (1982), Mahmood Hasan Khan (1982), Ziaul Haque (1981), Umar Chapra (1981), Mohammad Iqbal Asaria (1982), Muhammad Akram Khan (1981), and Volker Nienhaus (1981)[10] – have helped me to focus attention on some fundamental issues, which I have addressed in the present work. Needless to say, none of these scholars shares any blame for any of the shortcomings of the analysis presented in this book. I am especially thankful to Professor Alamgir Hashmi, who painstakingly went through the manuscript and made valuable editorial suggestions and improvements. I also wish to record my appreciation for the excellent typing by my Secretary, Muhammad Aslam.

Perhaps my greatest debt of gratitude is to my deceased parents, Syed Mohammad and Hasan Fatima, to my stepmother, Hamid Fatima, to my late uncle and aunt, Syed Mustafa

PREFACE

Hasan and Haideri Begum, and to my younger sister, Nasim Zehra, who helped me in acquiring a sympathetic view of society. My wife, Saeeda, and our four daughters, to whom this book is dedicated, helped me a great deal in forming my views about social processes.

Syed Nawab Haider Naqvi

June, 1992

NOTES

1 This does *not* mean that all else is unimportant in this regard.
2 As explained later in this book, such a desire to do good to others even at the cost of one's own welfare signifies *commitment*, rather than unadulterated self-interest maximization, as an *ideal* rule of economic behaviour. It does not necessarily mean that *actual* behaviour in a typical Muslim society will be a model of altruism and rectitude; for if that was the case, many interesting economic problems would not exist in such a society!
3 In the Islamic view of ethics, when institutions are not based on Equilibrium (*al 'Adl wal Ihsan*), they represent a state of Disequilibrium (*Zulm*).
4 Boisard (1987) makes the same point: '... the fusion of the spiritual and the temporal is such a constantly asserted factor [in Muslim societies] that ... one can understand the nature of man by deduction from Islam's juridical and moral laws' (p. 95).
5 The Prophet had warned against extreme (*involuntary*) poverty because it can lead man astray.
6 Since then the book has been translated into Persian, Indonesian, and Malaysian. It has also been adopted as an advanced textbook in many universities in Pakistan and abroad.
7 The statement in the text contrasts sharply with the existing literature on Islamic economics, according to which the subject is all about describing the ideal Islamic situation. To some extent, my own earlier work e.g., Naqvi (1981a; 1981b) – took the traditional position. I was concerned about the existence of an *Islamic* economy exclusively at the logical plane; but I was careful enough to note, especially in Naqvi (1981b), that what we were talking about was an essay in Islamic economic *philosophy*, as deduced from its ethical perceptions.
8 Indeed, most Muslim economists and scholars have written in the *belief* that the principles of Islamic economics are universal truths, requiring no refutation or confirmation. But, as argued in the text, such a belief will not permit the development of Islamic economics as a scientific, empirically verifiable, discipline.
9 The general approach of Baqir Sadr's *magnum opus* is similar to that followed in this book of seeing Islamic economics as inseparable from Islamic ethics; but he has not used the axiomatic approach

followed in this book, nor does he look upon Muslim society as a real-life counterpart of Islamic economics. (The relevant works of the authors mentioned in the text are cited at appropriate places in this book.)

10 See also my rejoinder to Nienhaus in Naqvi (1982).

1
INTRODUCTION

Philosophically speaking, an individual is a unified person moved to action by impulses that do not distinguish between the mundane and the spiritual. Thus, the somewhat oversharp division of man's activity into this-worldly and the other-worldly seems arbitrary and perhaps no better than a ploy to resolve the conflicting demands of specific religious, political or economic situations; it cannot be justified as a universal rule holding in all situations. According to the Islamic vision, the distinction between the secular and the spiritual is both pointless and counter-productive – pointless, because it is artificial and unreal; counterproductive, because it breeds schizophrenic tensions. It also makes men profess what they do not believe in, something that deprives them of the right value perspective.[1]

The unitary character of Islamic philosophy destroys the dichotomy between the secular and the spiritual both at the level of the individual and the society. At the level of the individual, man is seen as a theomorphic being. Man is free; but he should also be committed to the betterment of the society. Thus, driven by a strong ethical impulse, he is supposed to discharge his social and economic responsibilities for his own good and that of the society. At the socio-economic level, the act of giving to the poor and the needy is linked directly with the efforts to attain spiritual ascension.[2] Creating a 'unified' framework of thought and action thus, Islam seeks to create the necessary preconditions for social harmony and economic progress.

The connection between man's desire to promote his own welfare and his longing to satisfy his spiritual urges makes the task of synthesizing ethical imperatives with economic actions not just a matter of intellectual curiosity. Once it is accepted that the influence of religious beliefs on man's day-to-day social and economic behaviour is significant in a typical Muslim society, then it is no longer possible to model the latter without the former.[3] In fact, 'Islamic economy is part of the religion of Islam which covers the various branches of life' [Sadr (1982)]. Thus, the Muslim economist is faced with a difficult intellectual enterprise. He must show that bringing ethical considerations, which are *based on religion*, explicitly into the economic calculus in no way fetters the spirit of enquiry, and that by conjoining these factors into a single analytical scheme he can make a net contribution to economic knowledge. He must also re-formulate the basic Islamic propositions, motivated as they are by an essentially 'rightist' philosophy, in the form of a set of refutable hypotheses capable of being tested potentially if not actually.[4]

The world has changed a great deal since the medieval Muslim philosophers wrote about economic matters. Notwithstanding our filial reverence for what they thought about the social reality in their times, their writings are only partially helpful in comprehending the complexities of the modern age because the production relations – and the social reality which they define – have undergone a sea-change. We may not just *reconstruct* their ideas to suit the requirements of the modern age; that would be conferring an unnatural degree of plasticity and universality on these ideas.[5] Instead, while making full use of modern knowledge, we must come up with altogether *new* ideas within the matrix of modern knowledge, cultural mores, and institutional structures. The fruits of knowledge, irrespective of who created it, must be shared by all mankind to make this world a better place to live in. A blind adherence to irrelevant anachronisms is a sure-fire prescription for deepening the intellectual stagnation that Muslim societies have suffered from for centuries now. As we must uphold the supremacy of reason in the conduct of our affairs, we should seek to harness Islam's power to synthesize diverse strands of thought and weave them into a recognizable pattern which is both familiar and original.[6]

To make a convincing case for the Islamic economic system, it will have to be shown that the fusion of ethics and economics will give it an edge over other economic systems. This will be a difficult task because the existing economic systems – capitalism, socialism, the welfare state – have succeeded in achieving high rates of economic growth and social (including distributive) justice to an extent that is unprecedented in human history. And now with the dismantling of the socialist (communist) system in the Soviet Union, capitalism is being offered as a panacea for all economic ills, irrespective of the constraints of time and space. To meet the intellectual challenge of proving that there *is* an alternative to these economic systems for Muslim societies, it will have to be demonstrated that an Islamic economic system is at least as effective in facing the perennial problems of want, poverty, and human degradation. Indeed, it will be highly dangerous *not* to bother about such a demonstration in a real-word context and merely contend that since the Islamic policy instruments carry the Divine approval, they must work perfectly under all circumstances. Islam does not offer any such guarantees. *An Islamic economic system is as much man-made as any other economic system; and its success also will be ensured by the universally accepted tests of survival.* One of these tests is the capacity of a real-world system to experiment and innovate to meet new social and economic challenges. Thus, evolving an economic system which satisfies the laws of social dynamics and the dictates of social justice will require a flexible response: to fight for individual liberty when faced with economic or political totalitarianism; but also to assert the principle of social welfare in the midst of market capitalism.

Thus, the research programme of Islamic economics will inevitably be eclectic. On the one hand, the contribution to the evolution of human societies made by reformist (indeed, revolutionary) movements in the West and the great advances made by economic science in modern times must be recognized by Muslim economists. On the other hand, due attention should be paid to the fact that what essentially runs counter to the Islamic ethical values cannot be included without modification in the Islamic framework of thought.[7] For instance, the uncompromising positivistic position of both the neoclassical economics and the Marxist economics will not be acceptable. More specifically, the exclusive reliance on the 'self-interest maximization assumption', which is taken as synonymous with *rational* behaviour and is absolutely basic to neoclassical economics, cannot be carried over in its pristine form into Islamic economics. [See Khan (1992)]. The same holds for numerous other propositions, the most important of which is the Pareto-optimality principle. Such postulates will have to be either discarded or suitably modified to take into account the pervasive influence of ethical considerations on man's economic behaviour in a Muslim society.

In going from the first principles of Islamic ethics to economics, it is important to be absolutely clear about the direction that Islamic economics must take in its next cycle of development; the attempt is to be aimed at an interdisciplinary link-up to bring economics, ethics, and religion into a single orbit of thought. Two points should be noted in this context. (a) In deducing basic statements about Islamic economics, which are inevitably a set of *value* judgements, we are not just insisting on *any* ethic, but one which is derived from the Islamic religion. (b) The ethical principles that we are looking for are *not* consequence-insensitive; instead, they pay due attention to the social consequences of the exercise of property rights by individuals, and prescribe corrective action in every situation of social injustice.

Thus, Islamic economics will have to develop simultaneously at two levels. First, it must reflect a clear recognition and understanding of the essence of what Islam's fundamental ethical values are in order to discover the touchstone by reference to which we can establish the Islamic (or un-Islamic) nature of the given economic principles. The next logical step is to turn these ethical values into operative axioms. Once such a logical system has been set up, the essentials of Islamic economics can be deduced. Second, using Muslim society as a *real-world* counterpart of *Islamic* economics, a series of hypotheses must be established about representative Muslim behaviour. To establish such hypotheses, which are empirically falsifiable and which also posit the Islamic premise of ethics joined with economics, is among the main objectives of this book.

Although much of this effort runs counter to the insistence by mainstream (positive) economics on a value-free economics, yet the scientific validity of our procedure is not in doubt. If man's ethical perceptions do influence his behaviour in the real world, it is difficult to sustain the proposition that economic behaviour can somehow remain *untainted* by ethics. One can, of course, derive mathematically neat and amoral economic theorems by accepting the self-interest maximization postulate, but that does not lessen one bit the doubt about the exclusivity of the efficiency-oriented principles to explain and predict the real world where ethical issues also matter. Thus, it is reasonable to assert that to simulate reality in a Muslim society, ethical considerations must be taken into account because the religious beliefs held by the members of such a society further strengthen the hold of ethics on man's mind and action. It is not a question of whether such an attitude is rational or not as judged by some 'objective' criterion; the important thing for the economic analyst is to recognize the *economic significance* of such ethico-religious beliefs.

It is important to bear in mind that when inter-systemic comparisons are made – and reasons are spelled out why an Islamic economic system will be preferred by *Muslims* to any other system, e.g., capitalism, socialism or the welfare state, such an enterprise is meaningful within the matrix of the Islamic system of beliefs; it is *not* necessarily a proof of the absolute superiority of an Islamic economic system to all other systems so that *even* non-Muslims will also prefer it.[8] However, this fact does not detract from the 'universality' of such a system; it only points to the essential relativity of all human knowledge – Islamic economics being no exception to this rule.[9]

PLAN OF WORK

The analysis presented in this study, which has been developed from Naqvi (1981), is elaborated in thirteen chapters. The *Second* chapter is foundational in that it brings out the meaning and significance of the new discipline of Islamic economics. It is clearly recognized that, notwithstanding its axiomatic character, the new discipline must also relate to the analysis of the economic behaviour of a 'representative' Muslim in a typical *Muslim* society. It is only in this way that at least some of its key propositions, deduced formally from ethical axioms, will have a chance, however remote, of being tested in the real world. This chapter also points to some of the methodological issues that arise once the need to verify the key propositions of Islamic economics empirically is recognized.

In chapters *Three* and *Four*, I have employed the basic concepts of mathematical logic to express the essentials of Islamic ethics as a set of axioms, which are then used to deduce the basic propositions of Islamic economics. These two chapters are fundamental, because all the logical 'statements' made in the rest of the book presume that the axiom system identified here is an adequate representation of Islam's ethical perceptions – in the sense that it is a comprehensive but a (non-trivial) minimum possible set; that it is logically consistent and independent; that it possesses predictive power; and that it adds to our understanding about the world of Islam. Although the fundamental ethical axioms have been set up as a logical system, these too are verifiable statements in the context of a Muslim society. We have set up the Islamic axiom system – consisting of Unity, Equilibrium, Free Will, and Responsibility – on the basis of the assertions and value judgements made in the Quran and the *Sunnah*, which, notwithstanding fine theological differences between different schools of thought, are universally regarded by Muslims as true and infallible guides to social and economic activities. Thus, while we have used an essentially deductive method to lay the foundations of Islamic economics, at least some of the propositions so arrived at should be testable, *if not actually tested*, in the real world. However, it should be noted that to demand for each and every postulate of Islamic economics, established through *a priori* reasoning, to be *actually* tested and empirically verified is to ask too much of any discipline.[10] The importance of a theory, or a discipline, is established by showing that it points out a significant problem, and that it increases understanding of the problem. As it does this, Islamic economics can happily live with any number of unverified, and unverifiable, economic statements.

The *Fifth* chapter, using the analytical tools forged in the previous chapters, seeks to deduce the basic propositions (statements) of Islamic economics. As is customary, a few hypotheses are posited at this stage to make transparent the full meaning and import of the four basic ethical axioms noted above. We formulate the concept of the 'allowability constraint' to clarify what an integration of economics with ethics implies for the utility-maximizing calculus; and a number of other basic ideas of Islamic economics are discussed at this stage. In particular, we show that the Pareto-optimality principle, which is the cornerstone of neoclassical (micro) economics, does not agree with Islamic economics. The same is true of Benthamite utilitarianism and also of libertarian non-consequentialism. None of these hypotheses can yield any meaningful distributive principle, which is a point of emphasis in Islamic economics.

INTRODUCTION

Inter-systemic comparisons – with capitalism, socialism, and the welfare state – are presented in the *Sixth* chapter in terms of the rules of Islamic ethics to distinguish and highlight the Islamic point of view. As such, this discussion is not exhaustive; *nor does it seek to establish the superiority of the Islamic economic system in a 'global' sense on the (wrong) premise that an Islamic system is demanded because capitalism, socialism or the welfare state have failed.* Also, we have been careful not to commit the logical mistake of comparing an idealized Islamic economic system with real-life economic systems, thereby comparing the *ideals* of one system with the *practice* of the other systems. What we hope to achieve, though, is a comparative analysis that will highlight the scope of inter-systemic borrowings keeping in view the points of similarity and dissimilarity. The analysis also makes clear why the (idealized) Islamic economic system cannot be a carbon-copy of any other (idealized) economic system. As stated earlier, the reason is that the Islamic economic system can be logically derived *only* from Islamic ethics, and *not* from the ethical (or non-ethical) postulates of any other economic system. One of the central concerns of this chapter, and indeed of the entire book, is to distinguish between individual freedom and the (Islamic) state's duty to regulate this freedom. Problems arise because Islam explicitly emphasizes the individual's birth-right to make a choice between various options open to him; but, at the same time, it also spells out a mechanism whereby the conflict situations arising from different individuals' exercising their rights can be resolved, as far as possible, through a process of mutual consultation. Thus, while the state does not have any inalienable *rights* in the sense that an individual has, it does have a *responsibility* to maximize social welfare by laying down rules and procedures to appropriately constrain the selfishness of a few (rich *and* powerful) individuals.

Once the Islamic economic system is shown to *exist*, this fact (of its existence) should suggest hard-core policy objectives and a corresponding set of policy instruments. These matters are discussed in the next five chapters.

The *Seventh* chapter lays down the basic objectives of the Islamic economy. The reasonableness of this particular choice of objectives has also been shown to follow from the axioms identified earlier. These objectives are: individual freedom, distributive justice, economic growth, universal education, and maximum (not necessarily 'full') employment.[11]

In chapters *Eight* to *Eleven*, we discuss the set of *policy instruments* which have the best chance of attaining the Islamic policy objectives. Since policy objectives cannot be meaningful without the availability of an adequate number of policy instruments, the Islamic character of this taxonomic equation has been made clear. We have been careful at this stage to note that none of the policy instruments chosen contravenes any of the *explicit* Islamic injunctions – e.g., *it is not possible to include* riba *in the list of policy instruments*. But, at the same time, it will be counterproductive to insist on transplanting each and every *Islamically legitimate principle* – e.g., *Mudaraba* (Profit-and-Loss Sharing) – into the modern financial and economic institutions without making certain adjustments in it, without ascertaining its contextual relevance, and without ascertaining the compatibility of the economic consequences of such transplantation with the ethical principles of Islam. Here, the challenges of the modern world will necessitate making many adjustments and amendments to implement the policy directives derived from the ethical principles.

This discussion brings us to the issues related to the extreme complexity of making a successful 'transition' – i.e., of translating the Divine message within the crucible of real-life institutions. These matters are discussed in Chapter Twelve. The concluding chapter brings together the main thread of the arguments of the previous chapters to make the following point: while the universality of the Islamic truths, based on the Quran and the *Sunnah*, cannot be challenged by the Muslims, this 'fact' should not be used to establish the universality, indeed timelessness, of the ideas of the great Muslim theologians and scholars who wrote in a totally different socio-economic set-up. This 'fact' should also not be used to diminish the importance of present-day scholars. Any effort to validate the truth of logical and empirical statements made about modern-day economies by reference to the utterances, however wise, of some scholar of antiquity is a hopeless task. It is also counter-productive because such a process of going back to the beginning of time to establish the Islamic credentials of each and every proposition of Islamic economics will pre-empt creative initiative. To respond to the challenges of the modern age, the constraints of

INTRODUCTION

the existing social institutions must be respected, bearing in mind that no sure-fire Islamic formula exists to solve all economic problems of a modern Muslim society.

NOTES

1 This is a situation that Islam strongly disapproves of: 'O you who believe, why do you profess what you do not practice' (61:2). Note that here, as elsewhere in the book, the first number in parenthesis indicates the relevant chapter of the Quran while the second number denotes the specific verse in that chapter. Throughout, the translations of the Quran by Ali (1984) and Pickthall (1979) have been used or drawn on as they generally convey the best sense.
2 The Quran is explicit on this: 'How will you comprehend what the steep ascent is? – To free a neck (from the burden of debt or slavery), or to feed in times of famine. The orphan near in relationship, or the poor in distress...' (90; 12–16).
3 Iqbal (1986) has remarked, 'It is the mysterious touch of the ideal that animates and sustains the real, and through it alone we can discover and affirm the ideal. With Islam the ideal and the real are not two opposing forces which cannot be reconciled'. (p. 7)
4 The latest experimentation with Islamization in many Muslim countries, especially in Iran and in Pakistan, does enable one to empirically test the viability of an economy with certain Islamic features.
5 Iqbal (1986) emphasized the need to *reconstruct* the contributions made by the Muslims in various domains of human knowledge. What we insist on in the text is the need to *create* new knowledge because the problematics of the modern world has changed drastically.
6 Nasr (1968) has pointed out: 'Islam was given providentially the power to synthesize and absorb what was in conformity with its perspective from previous civilizations' (p. 36).
7 Gibb's observation is apt: 'The question is not one of refurbishing a time-encrusted methodology, nor on the other hand of transporting utilitarian/or humanistic ethics into Islam from other systems. It is a question of the spiritual roots of life and action...' [Gibb (1968), p. 131].
8 This follows because the basic propositions of any 'complete' logical construct, not only of economics, are formally correct only within the matrix of such a system. For instance, even a 'universal' truth that 'the sum of three angles of a triangle is equal to two right angles' is valid only within the Euclidean geometrical framework; it is false in the context of, say, spherical geometry.
9 In the tradition of Western economics, Marx (1977) was the first to point out the relativity of economic laws to particular economic regimes.
10 According to near-unanimous opinion among economists, such an insistence on the empirical verifiability of the basic postulates is not

necessary in the context of (modern) economics, which has been deduced from empirically *non-verifiable* postulates. But in the context of Islamic economics, such a demand can be adequately met – a decided advantage from the methodological point of view.

11 In Naqvi (1981), I did not include 'individual freedom' as a separate policy objective.

Part I
FOUNDATIONAL ISSUES

2
THE NATURE AND SIGNIFICANCE OF ISLAMIC ECONOMICS[1]

Islamic economics is about the representative Muslim's behaviour in a typical Muslim society. This might sound like *positive* economics, but that would be a misnomer because our discipline is normative by its very temperament – i.e., not restricted to making factual judgements alone, it is free to use value judgements, especially those based on religion. Thus, the fact that Islam's ethical perception is reflected in the economic statements about Muslim society does not in any way diminish the objective validity of these statements. On the other hand, such a perception provides the correct value perspective by reference to which the 'truth' of such statements can be established. This position is no less scientific than that taken by positive (neoclassical) economics, which insists on making specific economic statements without reference to ethics. Indeed, the explicit recognition of the value-laden character of Islamic economics makes it richer in content in that it encompasses a wider range of economic phenomena than does neoclassical economics. Another aspect of our definition is that it focuses on a real-life Muslim economy as opposed to a utopian Islamic economy, the main concern being the study of economic behaviour of a representative Muslim who may not be an ideal Muslim. Thus, the statements of Islamic economics, and the basic ethical axioms from which these statements are formally deduced, are essentially verifiable – or falsifiable.

A MATTER OF DEFINITION

Defining the subject-matter of Islamic economics in this manner constitutes a radical departure from the existing practice among the economists writing about Islamic economics.[2] A little reflection, however, should show that there is no other way of defining the new discipline. First, our definition envisages a 'counterfactual', wherein the basic Islamic ethical postulates and the economic statements deduced from them interact with the reality of the Islamic society. Then, within the context of the same counterfactual, the concept of a real-life Muslim society transforms essentially irrefutable economic and ethical assertions into *falsifiable* statements, without implying that the ethical postulates themselves or the resulting economic statements will *in fact* be falsified.[3] Second, it is important to study the behaviour patterns of economic agents in a Muslim society. Once this is done, new vistas of thought and action will open up for the growth of Islamic economics because from the process of examining the reciprocal problems of translating ideas into reality, and of allowing reality to reflect back on ideas, a realistic view will emerge about the *implementability* of such ideas. Third, by relating the behaviour of economic agents to a Muslim society, we are making the somewhat restrictive claim about Islamic economics; that its basic statements are not universal but relative to the 'reality' of the Muslim society as seen from a spatial as well as a temporal angle. The reason for limiting the scope of our discipline in this manner is that, while Islam's message, like that of the other religions, is universal, there is also an element of particularity about it, which must be recognized.

The central idea that defines Islamic economics, and which sets it apart from positive (neoclassical) economics, is its insistence on the *explicit* inclusion of an ethics *based on religion* in a unified analytical framework.[4] But, apart from establishing the philosophical validity of this idea from an Islamic point of view, it should be possible at least to relate it to real-life situations to be able to claim the objective validity of specific statements about Islamic economics. This is because such statements, which consist of both factual judgements and value judgements, can be shown as consistent with the 'facts' of a Muslim society. The two key concepts introduced below for this purpose are the Divine Presence and the real-life *Muslim* society (as distinct from an ideal *Islamic* society). Both these concepts are essentially empirical propositions in the sense that they can be factually verified as true or false.

ETHICS AND ECONOMICS

(i) The Belief in the Divine Presence

The representative Muslim's belief in the Divine Presence – 'Act. God will see your conduct' (9:105) – *and* his acting more or less in accordance with this belief is the key to an understanding of the decisive influence of ethics on economic behaviour. Indeed, a typical Muslim, with no special claims to piety, seriously believes that he is in direct communion with God, Who listens to his entreaties and rewards (punishes) him for his good (bad) actions. Knowing this, he seeks God's help in every significant move he contemplates – by saying *Inshaallah* (God Willing) each time he mentions his plans for a new enterprise.[5] And in a substantial number of actions – e.g., feeding the poor, giving alms, helping an orphan, generally *not* charging interest on loans among friends and relatives, not hoarding food items, and in the aversion to gambling and betting – seeking God's pleasure is the *mainspring* of economic action. It is under the influence of a firm belief in the Divine Presence that certain potent ideas – e.g., those about the equality of all men before God, about the poor having a right in the rich man's wealth *because* all wealth belongs to Allah, about a rich man's obligation to spend with moderation *because* he is a trustee not an owner of his wealth, about man being essentially a free agent with definite social responsibilities to discharge, etc. – are routinely believed in by the Muslims; and, to some extent, also practised, though not always consciously.[6] Such a belief also explains the tremendous appeal of the Shari'a (Divine Law) as 'an effective instrument to energize the demand for social justice' [Gibb (1968)]; as, for instance, feudal structures and practices in various Muslim societies have been opposed by many ulema on strictly religious grounds.

The *analytical* importance of the concept of the Divine Presence for Islamic economics should now be obvious. First, the integration of ethical imperatives with economic considerations takes place at the level of primary motivation of the representative Muslim in a more or less routine fashion, so that he hardly ever reasons about it; he simply *does* it. Second, such an amalgam of ethics and economics is an empirically verifiable – or, at least, falsifiable – 'fact', the importance of which is apparent not only at the level of philosophical discourse but also in the representative Muslim's day-to-day life.[7] Thus, it is possible to ascertain this 'fact' by generating the relevant information in various ways about how an ordinary Muslim typically behaves. Third, when considerations like the thought of the Hereafter play a significant role in man's daily life, his calculus of the 'profitable' course of action will accord due weight to non-monetary benefits (costs) as well. Thus, what may appear as an irrational action to a 'non-believer' becomes the hallmark of rationality to the 'believer'. Fourth, once the importance of this 'fact' is established, either by casual empiricism or more systematically, it is no longer legitimate to ignore the importance of ethical influence on man's economic behaviour.

It may be noted that, for analytical purposes, the representative Muslim is not required to *actually*, and faithfully, practise everything that he believes in or talks about. Indeed, if this was the case – if actual behaviour was exactly, or even approximately, like ideal behaviour – then there would be nothing left to 'explain'. Thus, the departure from the ideal norms may be frequent, even systematic; but that does not detract from the importance of a norm being used as a reference point, and as a guide to action.[8]

(ii) Muslim Society versus the Islamic Society

For the concept of the Divine Presence to exercise a significant quantitative influence, it must be a *universally* held concept in the given society. Once this condition is satisfied, the concept becomes important from an *economic* point of view – namely, *as a real-life counterpart of Islamic economics*, and as a virtual laboratory for testing specific statements of Islamic economics. This is important because without such a physical reality, the statements of Islamic economics will be no more than a collection of non-falsifiable assertions of a philosophical nature,[9] and the entire procedure of deducing economic statements from a set of ethical beliefs will become suspect. From the scientific point of view, the situation is not made any more plausible by calling one's attention to the fact that such an ideal society once existed during the time of the Prophet and the first four caliphs; because while that society is a model for Muslims, it cannot serve as a real-life counterpart of Islamic economics.[10]

It should be noted that we are *not* asserting that all hypotheses of Islamic economics should be *inductively* generated. That *never* happens in the world of science, much less in the case of economics, where most hypotheses are mere simplifications about the real world, and the logical predictions of which are hardly ever confronted with reality.[11] All that we claim is that, as long as there is a real-life counterpart, the statements of Islamic economics can be tested empirically *some day*.

ON ASSESSING ISLAMIC ECONOMICS

The assertion that the key concepts of Islamic economics are empirically testable leads to the question: Can general statements, about it be 'observed' in the real world? One may be tempted to answer that the physical existence of the Muslim society should make possible a *sensory* confirmation of such statements. But, alas, this answer is *not* adequate. The reason is that it is not possible to make general statements on the basis of singular (specific) statements which *alone* are observable. Specifically, the case is *not* that general propositions of Islamic economics can be constructed, brick by brick, from observations – i.e., singular statements – pertaining to the real world.[12] The physical existence of the Muslim society is not sufficient by itself to confirm statements about Islamic economics by just *looking around*. Hence, strictly speaking, *sensory* confirmation is an unreasonable – indeed, impossible – demand to make to justify the existence of Islamic economics as a separate discipline.[13]

The fact of the matter is that in the case of Islamic economics – even more than is the case with positive economics – the problem of assessment can at best be handled in a somewhat *ad hoc* fashion. There will be cases where the basic hypotheses are mere simplifications based on the most tentative type of empiricism; or when the predictions based on such hypotheses are seldom confronted with reality; or when the hypotheses are not formulated in a testable form. Thus, Islamic economics will also have its share of the excess baggage of *non-tested* statements and theories, with the hope that it will be possible to formulate them in a testable way.[14]

It is of utmost importance that, when the opportunity arises, the community of Muslim economists is ready to confront the prevailing conception of reality with their own theories, most of which will be drawn from some basic ethical axioms; even more, they should be prepared to modify, even discard, at least some of their own theoretical idealizations once they are empirically falsified. But if, instead, we make excuses each time we run into trouble with our theories, then there will be no scientific progress made in Islamic economics.[15] Thus, it is essential that the evidence becoming available from the experiences of modern Muslim societies is taken into account – not dismissed as irrelevant – to test the propositions of our discipline. In particular, it needs to be pointed out that it will not help matters at all if each and every proposition of Islamic economics is considered sacrosanct, beyond empirical testing.

Another relevant methodological point is that, according to the widely held opinion among economists, what counts is the empirical testing of the *consequences* of the basic postulates, which themselves need not be tested. Even here, the requirement applies not to each and every statement deduced from the basic postulates, but only to a conjunction of logically independent propositions.[16] In the present context, it is not necessary to test the ethical axioms; but only a collection of individual statements derived from these. However, in contrast to positive economics, Islamic economics should perhaps satisfy even the 'ultra-empiricists' because, as noted above, a pale shadow of the Islamic ethical axioms can be observed in the day-to-day behaviour of the Muslims.

DOES ISLAMIC ECONOMICS EXIST?

We can now address the fundamental question about the existence of Islamic economics as a separate discipline. The preceding discussion has led us to an affirmative answer to this question. In this section, we examine the views of those who *believe* in the universality of the economic science – the so-called monoeconomists – and who, mostly for aesthetic reasons, hold that there is only one economics which is neoclassical economics. They would, thus, look askance at any effort to construct Islamic economics because it would be a sacrilege against a 'unified' neoclassical economic theory, and also because it would be non-secular.[17] [Khan (1991, 1992)]. Then, there are the 'insider's' denials about Islamic economics – 'that Islamic economics is not a science' – on the ground that a true Islamic economy does not actually exist yet to allow the researcher to establish certain general laws; and also because the Islamic view of economics is inextricably bound with its social, cultural, and religious views. (See Sadr [1982, Ch. 4]). Among other things, this view implies that present-day Muslim societies cannot be used as a basis for a generalization about Islamic economics because of their manifest imperfections relative to the Islamic ideals.

Each of these arguments needs careful examination.

It is now widely understood that economic laws, despite their generality, derive their distinctive character from the structure of society and, in that sense, are not absolute truths.[18] They are relative truths, both over time and space, and across different societies at different stages of development. They are also relative to a variety of social mores, cultural norms, and sets of beliefs held by economic agents. If, according to Weber (1949), the purpose of the social sciences is ultimately to gain an understanding about the real world, then we must be ready to get out of the straitjacket of a universal economic science and admit the possibility of other types of economics, which may be able to address the relevant issues and provide an adequate framework for their solution.[19] But these different types of economics need not be closeted in watertight compartments; indeed, to make progress, there must be enough room for a cross-fertilization of ideas between them.

Another source of doubt about the subject-matter of Islamic economics is its explicit use of ethical propositions as a basis of statements about the economic universe. Thus, instead of factual and *positive* statements, which claim objective validity, what we have in Islamic economics is a combination of positive judgements and value judgements – even as the dividing line between the two is at best fuzzy. In what sense is then our discipline scientific? In other words, how can the validity of a value judgement be tested against 'facts'? As Harsanyi (1989) points out, this can be done – value judgements proven objectively invalid – if 'they are contrary to the facts or because they are based on the wrong value perspective.' Now the twin concepts of the Divine Presence and the Muslim society provide a basis for checking such judgements against facts, while the ethical axioms form a 'value perspective' against which the objective validity of value judgements can be tested.

Finally, the existence of a Muslim society – which forms about one-fifth of the world's population, has distinctive characteristics of its own, and occupies a very large geographical area – justifies Islamic economics as a separate discipline in its own right. There is nothing unscientific about such an assertion because the laws of economics lack the absoluteness of the physical laws. Instead, they are formed, and changed, in response to the changes in the nature of society [Zamagni (1989)].[20] The reassertion in the Muslim world to live a life according to the Islamic precepts poses a challenge to which Muslim economists must respond – and, to some extent, they already have done so by explicitly incorporating religio-ethical values into the corpus of mainstream economics.[21]

SUMMARY

In sum, Islamic economics is a study of the representative Muslim's economic behaviour in a modern Muslim society. It is normative by its very composition; *not* of the positive type as neoclassical economics. Robbins's attempt to effect a divorce between ethics and economics is not recognized by some as 'legal' even in modern economics [Harsanyi (1989)]. But such attempts are totally misplaced in Islamic economics because of its insistence on *explicit* inclusion of ethical values into the economic calculus – i.e., accepting religion (Islam) as the source of such ethical values. Like neoclassical economics, it relates the ends to the 'scarce means which have alternative uses'; indeed, it does so more effectively because of its refusal to equate rational behaviour with self-interest maximization. Also, the recognition of ethical imperatives reduces the transaction costs of the pursuits of economic agents by absorbing a lesser amount of real resources.[22] And, notwithstanding the many imperfections of a Muslim society from a religious point of view – and which society is perfect in that sense? – the members of such a society do reflect the Islamic ethical and religious values in their daily lives. With such a society existing, there is scope for empirically testing the 'truth' of various statements of Islamic economics.

While we proceed in this study with the assurance that Islamic economics exists not only at the logical level but also has its real-world counterpart in a Muslim society, we must adopt a critical attitude towards our discipline. We should be ready to question the truth of specific statements of Islamic economics; and consider them as falsifiable statements open to an ongoing re-examination in the light of new empirical evidence. Islamic economics will not make any progress at all if its practitioners do not question the validity of specific statements of their discipline. Indeed, we must give up illusions about the infallibility of each and every propositions of Islamic economics just because it is Islamic, and shed a lot of excess baggage as Islamic economics is assessed by testing the rules of economic behaviour, which have been derived from the first principles of Islamic ethical axioms. Such a procedure will also entail an empirical testing of specific statements, however tentative the effort. But, most of all, we must address the subject of Islamic economics as social scientists, and not as religious enthusiasts. The *relativity*, and the *changeability*, of the basic propositions of Islamic economics must be the watchword.

NOTES

1 The title of this chapter, 'inspired' by L. Robbins's classic (1932), is designed to highlight the difference in the approaches between positive (neoclassical) economics and Islamic economics with respect to the importance of ethics in the latter. While Robbins and other neoclassical economists refuse any other role for ethics, Islamic economists consider it absolutely central to valid economic statement.
2 In my book: *Ethics and Economics* (1981), I too had stated that the Islamic economic system existed at the logical plane only. Thus, I tended to treat the subject in most of my writings as an Islamic economic *philosophy*. In doing so, I followed the practice of numerous notable thinkers and economists writing on the subject, who disregard the modern Muslim societies as real-world counterparts of Islamic economics.
3 The italicised portions in the text highlight the basic character of the scientific statement — i.e., to qualify as a scientific statement, it is not at all required that it has 'in fact been tested'; all that is required of it is that it is 'capable of being tested.' See Popper (1980) (p. 48).
4 The same remarks will also apply to Marxian economics, which insists on a separation of economics from ethics to demonstrate the 'scientific' nature of socialism.
5 Thus, Bell (1953) remarks: 'No book has exercised a deeper influence upon the spirit of man than the Quran ... It is the basis of [Muslims] religious beliefs, their ritual, and their law; *the guide of their conduct, both public and private*. It moulds their thought and its phrases enter into their literature and their daily speech.' (p. 1).
6 Thus, Boisard (1987) remarks: 'The intimate idea which the [Muslim]

believer has of God is interesting and fundamental, inasmuch as it determines his individual actions and, consequently, the social life of the community.' (p. 31). Hashmi (1986) has made a similar point in the context of Muslim literature: "these [Muslim] societies are essentially linked to the spirit of Islam as their separate lives are subsumed by this 'complete code of life" ' (p. 4).

7 A relevant example is the widespread practice of the giving of *Zakat* and other religious dues on a voluntary basis even by those Muslim businessmen who may feel no qualms about evading (a 'secular') income tax!

8 The contents of footnote 2 are also relevant here.

9 A fine point of logic is in order here. While all scientific (empirical) statements are generated from a set of general principles or axioms, which themselves need not be empirically testable, it should be possible, even if only as a theoretical possibility, to *falsify* the general principles by 'singular' statements (descriptions) about the real world.

10 In other words, the said period in Muslim history is more a part of the *model* than altogether of the reality.

11 Two outstanding examples of such 'cases' in the mainstream (positive) economics are the following: (a) The real-life significance of increasing and decreasing returns, which played such a crucial role in Ricardian (classical) economics, was never established empirically even though dire predictions continued about natural resources scarcities. (b) The timeless Cobb-Douglas Production Function has been freely used to make basically empirical statements about the historical sequence of events in the real world – e.g., the explanation about the constancy of the relative shares of labour and capital. There are many other such *non-verified* (but not *non-verifiable*) propositions in positive economics which lay a claim to the universal empirical validity of its key propositions. See Blaug (1985), especially chapter 17.

12 The statement in the text is consistent with the (correct) logical position that, while general statements cannot be *verified* by (positive) singular statements, the former type can be *falsified* by the latter type of (negative) statements. See Popper (1980), Chapter 4.

13 The problem of deducing general (universal) statements from singular (specific) statements is known as *Hume's problem of induction*, as owed to Hume (c. 1748). It is known to be insoluble. It follows that the only way to create *empirical* statements is to *deduce* particular statements from general statements. Popper (1980) refers to this procedure as the *deductive method of testing*, that 'a hypothesis can only be empirically tested – and only *after* it has been advanced' (p. 30). It may be noted that many a great philosopher of science, like Wittgenstein, has insisted on the *inductive* method of constructing empirical hypotheses – according to which every meaningful proposition is reducible to elementary propositions, which are the 'pictures of reality'. But in the text, following Popper, we reject this as a valid way of generating scientific propositions.

14 Blaug (1985) suggests that 'a theory is not to be condemned just because it is not as yet testable, not even if it is so framed as to preclude testing, provided it draws attention to a significant problem and provides a framework for its discussion from which a testable implication may some day emerge' (p. 703).
15 Some of these matters have been discussed generally in Hausman (1984).
16 Machlup (1956) calls this method of assessment as that of 'indirect testing', which does not require that the basic postulates – e.g., the profit-maximization postulate, on which a significant portion of neoclassical economics rests – be subjected to empirical testing. Those who insist on testing even the basic postulates are referred to as the ultra-empiricists; but these purists of the profession are in a minority.
17 See Khan (1991) (1992b) on this. It may be interesting to note that such objections have also been raised about the discipline of development economics, the existence of which has been fervently denied by neoclassical economists. See Naqvi (1993) for a critical survey of these controversies.
18 Deane (1983) has noted: 'There is no one kind of truth which holds the key to the fruitful analysis of all economic problems, no pure economic theory that is immune to changes in social values or current policy problems' (p. 11). Thus Arrow (1985) asks the basic question: 'Is economics a subject like Physics, true for all times or are its laws historically conditioned?' – and suggests that probably the latter is the case.
19 It may be noted that there are already four types of economics existing side by side, albeit not always peacefully – neoclassical economics, Marxian economics, institutional economics, and development economics.
20 As a rule, the growth of economic science owes more to the exogenous factors than to the factors endogenous to the discipline. One of the most remarkable examples of exogenous compulsions leading to a sea-change in the realm of economics is the Keynesian Revolution, which was directly prompted by the Great Depression. That it was not endogenously motivated can be seen from the fact that neoclassical micro-economics to this day shows no traces of the Keynesian 'heresy'!
21 It is generally felt that the response to this challenge from Western economists, in all probability, will be a rather weak one, if not one that is downright negative or even contemptuous.
22 One implication of accepting Robbins's broad characterization of economic activity is that we firmly reject as meaningless the assertion made by some Muslim thinkers that Islamic economics deals with the plenitude of (physical) resources instead of with the fact of their scarcity. It is a simple universal fact that in relation to the human wants, the resources must *always* be scarce.

3
THE ETHICAL FOUNDATIONS

An essential first step in deducing the rules of economic behaviour in the Islamic economy is to construct a 'representative' axiom system that captures adequately the spirit of Islamic ethics and forms the basis of meaningful economic statements. There are at least four reasons for taking this step. First, the basic religious and moral precepts of Islam should be taken as a minimal set of axioms to make logically valid statements about economic behaviour in the Islamic society. Second, in the context of the Islamic society, just any *ethical* perception will not do. Only an ethical system based on the Islamic *religion* qualifies to be taken into account in determining the broad contours of Islamic economics. This is so not only because the Islamic ethical view of life processes claims 'completeness' and 'consistency', but also because this view draws strength from a set of universally held Islamic beliefs. Third, this analytical strategy highlights the central normative characteristics of Islamic economics: it admits value judgements as statements which are objectively valid about a Muslim society, where economic behaviour cannot be seen in isolation from ethical norms.

In this chapter, we present a comprehensive ethical axiom system which adequately summarises Islam's deontological perception of life-processes.[1] In the next chapter, we take up the question of the adequacy of these axioms as a tool of economic analysis.

AN OUTLINE OF ISLAMIC ETHICS

The central point of Islamic ethics is to determine man's freedom to act and his responsibility given his belief in Divine omnipotence. If man is given absolute freedom of will, then God's' omnipotence is compromised. On the other hand, if the belief is exclusively focused on God's omnipotence, then man's responsibility for his actions, or the eschatological foundation of religion, becomes meaningless.[2] In the Islamic ethical scheme, man is the cynosure of God's creation. He is God's vicegerent (*Khalifa*) on Earth: 'He it is Who hath placed you as vicegerent of the earth . . .' (6:166). Hence, the entire purpose of man's life is to realize his viceregal virtuality as a 'free' agent invested with a Free Will,[3] able to make a choice between good and evil, right or wrong. By virtue of his freedom, man can *either* realize his theomorphic virtuality of being God's vicegerent on earth or deny himself this exalted niche by making the wrong choice. In other words, man will be held accountable for the choices he makes in his individual capacity.

Every man combines in himself both an 'individual man' and a 'collective man', and there is an essential reciprocity between these two facets of man's personality. His (undivided) individuality highlights his freedom; but his being a collectivity at the same time makes him responsible to the society. Far from inducing any schizophrenic morbidity, this essential duality of man's nature fortifies him from within.[4] Armed with a cause, he is well-placed to reach out to his viceregal ideal by submitting himself without reserve to God's will. As one ever engaged in a constructive struggle to achieve a higher mission in life, man is never 'alienated' from his environment.[5] Another distinctive characteristic of the Islamic view is that it leaves enough 'elbow room' to accommodate under one roof, so to speak, both man's soaring idealism to take him to a spiritual ascent and his mundane concern for his personal well-being. The 'space' between the ideal and the reality is filled by the quality of *'Adl* and *Ihsan* (i.e., Equilibrium), of which social justice is only one aspect. According to this quality, everything is assigned a proper place. Not only that; if anything is *not* assigned its proper place, then the aim of a free and responsible man must be to rectify this undesirable state of affairs by achieving balance (*mizan*) and equity (*qist*).

A key element of man's freedom – and his concomitant responsibility to the society – is that both these concepts flow from a Muslim's belief in God's unrivalled supremacy in the universe and beyond. According to the Quran, this belief is *the* reason why all men are free and equal: '... that none of us take any others for lord apart from God' (3:64). This definition of freedom as an essentially ethical proposition adds a new dimension to it. Not only is the political and economic freedom meant here but also a freedom from avarice and greed: 'Whoever preserves himself from his own greed will be prosperous' (59:9). Seen from this angle, it should be clear that man's political, social, and economic freedoms are nothing but expressions of Islam's ethical perceptions about man and society.

THE ETHICAL AXIOMS

The Islamic vision of man in relation to himself and his social environment is representable by four ethical axioms – Unity, Equilibrium, Free Will, and Responsibility – which together form an irreducible, non-trivial set. Although each of these axioms has been variously emphasized in Muslim history, yet a broad consensus has evolved in our own time about their cumulative import for Muslim socio-economic perspective.[6]

Unity (*Tawhid*)

The ultimate source of Islamic ethics is the unqualified and unalloyed belief in God's Unity. It particularly denotes the *vertical* dimension of Islam – linking the imperfect and finite social institutions with a Perfect and Infinite Being. This link-up is effected by man's unconditional surrender before Him, by making his desires, ambitions, and actions subservient to His command: 'Tell them: "My service and Sacrifice, my life and my death, are all of them for God, the creator and Lord of all the worlds"'(6:162). Man's submission to God helps man to realize his theormorphic potentiality;[7] it also releases him from human bondage. By integrating the political, economic, social, and religious aspects, man's life is transformed into a homogeneous whole, consistent from within and integrated with the vast Universe without. Thus, man achieves social harmony by promoting a sense of belonging to a universal brotherhood.

It should be particularly noted that the Islamic unitary worldview is not restricted to a society of Muslims alone but extends to the entire humanity deemed as one society: 'O man, We created you from a male and female, and formed you into nations and tribes that you may recognise each other' (49:13). Thus, the knowledge of one's self, of one's fellow beings, and of other nations produces a harmonious world by promoting toleration of dissent.

The integrative social role of Unity[8] flows from an awareness, especially in Muslim society, of God's Omnipotence: 'He has certainly power over every thing' (35:1); of His Knowledge of all things: 'Allah is Knower of all Things" (5:177); and of His Ownership of all things: 'To God belong the heavens and the earth . . .' (3:180). And yet, in such an absolutist world, man's freedom is also ensured. It flows from His being also the Judge of human action: 'Is not God the most equitable of all judges' (95:8).[9] Whence follows the Islamic concept of the freedom of man. However, it should be carefully noted that this concept is not meant to dilute human freedom, but only to point out the 'best' way of exercising it. Thus, man is free to own, but the best pattern of ownership is to consider it as a virtual *trusteeship* of what truly belongs to God – and takes place according to the Divine Law. But once these Divine Laws are obeyed, man's ownership of property and other things is practically absolute. Such a perspective acts as the central *catalytic* force in the Islamic society and acts *on* the individual and *through* the individual. This force, which derives its strength from a deep sense of the Divine Presence, transforms man's love for himself into a love for God's creation.[10] Thus, an abiding concern for ethical fulfilment raises the level of the individual's consciousness, in a vertical direction to a higher plane of consciousness, by adding the force of voluntarism to the altruistic instincts of man.

Equilibrium (*Al 'Adl wal Ihsan*)

Corresponding to Unity, the twin Islamic concepts of *al 'Adl* and *al Ihsan* denote a state of social Equilibrium.[11] The Quran states: 'Verily God has enjoined justice and kindness' (16:90). As a social ideal, the principle of Equilibrium provides for a complete description of all the virtues of the basic set of social institutions – legal, political, and economic. On the economic plane, the principle defines a first-best configuration of the production, consumption, and distribution activities,[12] with the clear understanding that the needs of all the least-privileged members in

Muslim society constitute the *first* charge on the real resources of the society.[13]

To understand the full social connotation of the Islamic concept of Equilibrium, it should be noted that the antonym of *al 'Adl* is *Zulm*, which denotes a social disequilibrium in the sense that the resources of the society flow *from* the poor *to* the rich. This is not allowed in Islam for the reason contained in the following verse of the Quran: 'So that it (i.e., wealth) does not concentrate in the hands of those who are rich among you' (59:7). Read together with the Quranic verse quoted earlier, it becomes obvious that, starting from a state of Disequilibrium, all steps must be taken to attain Equilibrium; that the 'rights' of the 'needy and the deprived' are restored to them through a fair distribution of income and wealth; and that this process should continue. Viewed thus, the principle of Equilibrium encompasses both the desirable state of affairs and the process to get there. Thus, when it is asserted that Islam insists on Equilibrium, such an assertion includes not only the exact point where the social and economic forces are perfectly balanced, but also the territory adjoining this point, where these forces are off-balance. But the condition is that a mechanism must be provided to restore, approximately if not exactly, the state of balance. Such an assertion also draws attention to the intertemporal dimension of this concept: a state of Disequilibrium today can be justified if it leads to Equilibrium tomorrow; and, contrarily, an insistence on Equilibrium at each instant of time may be held unjustifiable if it leads to Disequilibrium in a dynamic context. An example of this principle is the justification of the inequality of income if it can be shown to accelerate growth through capital accumulation; and, conversely, equality today may be unjustified if it slows down economic growth through capital consumption. The point is that despite an air of absolutism that surrounds moral precepts, their correct application requires an awareness of their actual context.

Corresponding to the vertical dimension of Islam denoted by Unity, Equilibrium constitutes its *horizontal* dimension.[14] It *requires* that the various elements of life be (re-)ordered to produce the 'best' economic dispensation.[15] Thus, while the quality of Equilibrium need *not* hold in the economic (sub-) space, willy-nilly, it must be established through purposive action.[16] It may be noted here that, unlike its usage in economics or mechanics, the term Equilibrium is distinctly normative in character.[17] As with Unity, the attribute of Equilibrium is also pre-figured in God Himself, who is also *al 'Adil*, the dispenser of Equilibrium. This is the reason why Equilibrium is a foundational ethical value, which summarises a large part of the Islamic ethical teachings – i.e., the desirability of an equitable distribution of income and wealth, the need for helping the poor and the needy, the necessity for making adjustments in the entire spectrum of consumption, production, and distribution relations, and so on. It also shows why this value signifies not only a desirable property of human institutions but also a definite recommendation that all human institutions must be *re-ordered* if they do not satisfy this value; and why, in most societal contexts, the insistence on maintaining an unjust *status quo*, especially that with respect to the structure of (private) property holdings, would be against the Islamic message. The reason is that such a status quo is *Zulm* both as a state of affairs and as a process so that its existence is inconsistent with a dynamic convergence of social forces to a state of perfect balance. Once this fact is established, the necessary corrective action also becomes *mandatory* from the Islamic point of view. Thus, if the existing structure of land holdings is feudalistic – i.e., it fails to accord priority to the interests of the cultivators of the soil over those of the non-cultivators – then it *must* be reformed to satisfy the Equilibrium axiom.

Free Will (*Ikhtiy'ar*)

In the Islamic perspective, man is *born* with a 'free will' – i.e., with the faculty of making a choice in various conflict situations. While man's freedom is both unrestricted and voluntary, so that he is free to make the wrong choice as well, it is in his own interest to make the 'right' choice: 'Say: O mankind! Now hath the Truth from your Lord come unto you. So whosoever is guided is guided for the good of his soul, and whosoever erreth erreth only against it.' (10:108). Indeed, God's blessings have been made conditional on man's *first* making the 'right' choice: 'Verily God does not change the state of a people till they change their inner selves...' (13:11). Thus, the *ethical* basis of man's freedom flows from the anatomy of making the 'right' choice.

It should be remembered that it is this faculty of making a

choice that makes man God's vicegerent (*Khalifa*) on earth, and which defines the central element of man's theomorphic character. Insofar as this viceregal stature denotes a virtuality rather than something that actually obtains, we come back to the question of how best to realize it. Another point of clarification is that, in the Islamic perspective, man is not chained to any historical determinism. While God is all-knowing, he is also the ultimate Judge of the manner in which man exercises his inborn right to choose between good and evil and other situations that lie between these polar extremes.

The key to an understanding of the ethical basis of individual freedom lies in grasping the fact that Divine Omniscience does *not* necessarily imply any Divine Responsibility to see to it that man does make the right choice, even though, if implored, Divine Mercy may do just that. Since man is free, he has only two options: *either* he, obeying the Divine Law, makes the right choice and is guided to the 'right path' *or* he makes the wrong choice and is led away from the 'right path' – and may even oppose God.[18] One may look upon the same matter in another way: man is free and potentially theomorphic but this potentiality is realized only under the umbrella of God's knowledge of what is best for man. But if man's actions do not conform to such knowledge, then that is a prescription for degradation and destruction in this world and in the Hereafter – an eventuality that has also been promised by God.

It may be noted that, at a philosophical level, the Islamic concept of autonomy is basically different from the contractarian concept of the absolute autonomy of the individual, who makes his own laws.[19] For instance, according to Kant, an individual is acting autonomously when he himself chooses the guiding principles of action as the most adequate expression of his being a free and rational person. On the other hand, the Islamic concept of individual freedom is properly understood as relative, since absolute freedom is only God's. Indeed, Islam rejects the *absolute* autonomy of man: '... but yet man is rebellious, for he thinks he is sufficient in himself' (96: 6–7). For instance, the individual's right to do as he pleases with private property is *not* unrestricted in Islam: to the non-believer's query related in the Quran, '... does your piety teach that we ... desist from doing what we like with our goods?' (11:87), the Islamic answer is emphatically in the affirmative.

While this philosophical difference between the Kantian and the Islamic points of view is important and should be duly noted, it is also important to remember that being relative does not in any way diminish the quality of individual freedom that Islam does grant.[20] Indeed, quantitatively and qualitatively, the Islamic (relative) freedom may even be greater than the Kantian absolute freedom; greater qualitatively because its exercise has greater depth and cutting power, flowing as it does from a deep moral conviction; greater quantitatively because it depends in an important way on man's freedom from avarice and greed for worldly possessions and from the slavery of the self.

The Islamic perception of human freedom is also diametrically opposed to the libertarian *non*-consequentialist moral philosophy; any social outcome, even the unjust one, must also be *socially* acceptable if it flows from the legitimate (legal) exercise of individual rights; and no effort should be made to 'pattern' such an outcome.[21] In sharp contrast, the Islamic view would emphasize 'patterning' the socially unjust outcome of individual action. To put the matter positively, the socially acceptable outcomes are those which improve the welfare of the least-privileged groups in society. Incidentally, in this sense, the Islamic position is nearer the Rawlsian Difference Principle, which judges the goodness of a state of affairs by reference to the welfare of the least-privileged people in society [Rawls (1971)].

To assert that man, in any given situation, is guided by rules and procedures based on the Divine Law does *not* necessarily mean that the element of *uncertainty* facing him in making the right choice will be any the less if he is guided by man-made laws; or that the demands on human ingenuity would be any the less than otherwise. *This is because the Divine Laws, with few exceptions, lay down only the general guidelines; but within the framework of these guidelines, careful intellection is required to interpret – and reinterpret – it within specific societal contexts, and to suit the needs of changing times.*[22]

Responsibility (*Fardh*)

Corresponding to Free Will is the Responsibility axiom. Although the two axioms come as a natural *pair*, yet it does *not* mean that the two are logically, or practically, so inter-related as to be indistinguishable from each other. Islam lays great emphasis on the concept of Responsibility; but this does *not* imply caring less about individual freedom. Instead, it seeks to establish a proper balance between the two. According to this view, modern civilization would be *defined* in terms of a series of steps to *constrain* individual freedom appropriately so that the inherent conflict between maximizing one's own interests is counter-balanced by the need to maximize social welfare – the dividing line between the individual and the society being necessarily *ad hoc* and shifting in accordance with the dictates of time.[23] Even, at a logical plane, individual freedom needs to be appropriately constrained because unlimited individual freedom implies unlimited responsibility, which is an absurdity as both these statements cannot be true at the same time.

The Islamic conception of Responsibility is comprehensively defined.[24] There are two fundamental aspects of this concept which should be noted at the outset. First, responsibility goes with man's viceregal status – his being God's *Khalifa* on earth. But, as noted above, this viceregal status is more a virtuality (potential state) than a fact (realized state). It takes considerable effort on man's part to ascend to this lofty station – indeed, it takes doing good *acts*, which mostly take the form of *giving* to the poor and the needy. Not only that; in doing good acts man may even give away what *he loves most* for himself: 'You will never come to piety unless you spend of things you love' (3:92). Thus, man secures his freedom – especially from avarice and greed – by discharging his responsibility to the poor in the society. Indeed, *not* discharging one's responsibility in this sense amounts to a denial of faith.[25]

Second, the Islamic concept of Responsibility is basically *voluntaristic* in nature and is not to be confused with the 'dictatorship solution', which Islam totally rejects. Thus, while this principle implies making a sacrifice, it is *not* the kind of sacrifice that one would consider a hardship. Instead, the act of giving is linked with the process of becoming a better person in the sense that 'he may grow (in virtue)' (92:18). This is something that an individual would consider to be in his own interest as the weight of moral and non-monetary consideration increases in consciousness.

Man has a responsibility towards God, to his own self, and to others. But these three facets of responsibility only underscore the central ethical principle that the individual, though possessing a distinctive personality of his own, becomes even more distinguished as an integral part of the totality of mankind. There is no virtue in withdrawing into splendid isolation in the pursuit of spiritual excellence, *because* the ascension of man is achieved by doing good to others, especially to the poor: 'How will you comprehend what the steep ascent is? – To free a neck (from the burden of debt or slavery), or to feed in times of famine. The orphan near in relationship, or the poor in distress...' (90:12–16).

The fact that he is an integral part of the society imposes a truly grave responsibility on the individual.[26] The Quran warns against insensitivity towards human suffering: 'What has come upon you that you fight not in the cause of God and for the oppressed, men, women and children who pray...' (4:75). It follows that (a free) man should be sensitive to his environment. Not only that; he must also be *sensitive* to the *consequences* of the exercise of his own rights (i.e., his own freedom). Even more, if harm is being done to the society – especially to the least privileged in the society – *either* through his own doings or by the doing of others, he must act positively. Thus, the doctrine of Responsibility is indeed a *dynamic* principle. If for any reason whatsoever an unjust social state comes to prevail, then it is man's responsibility to change it to the extent that it is feasible for him to do so.

We may also note what man is *not* responsible for. First, man is not responsible for what others do: 'Each soul earns (what it earns) for itself, and no man shall bear another's burden' (6:164). Second, man is not held accountable for what his forefathers did in the past: 'Those were the people, and they have passed away. Theirs is the reward for what they did, as yours will be for what you do. You will not be questioned about their deeds' (2:134). Thus, freed from the chains of an irrelevant past, man is required to act positively in the present and in the future. Third, man's responsibility is in proportion to his financial and physical capacity to bear it. In some cases, an individual is absolved of his responsibility because someone else who is better equipped than he is to perform this duty. This is referred to as *Fard 'ala al-Kifaya* in the Islamic ethical literature.[27] Fourth, one man's responsibility ends where another man's freedom begins. Thus, in the discharge of one's responsibility, man should be careful to exercise it with moderation and good judgement. It is not for any individual to decide for himself what is good for others, and for the society. He must abide by social norms of good behaviour; and must respect other individuals' rights in discharging his own social responsibility.

SUMMARY

In the scheme of Islamic ethics, a free man establishes three simultaneous relationships; with God, with his own self, and with the society. The four basic axioms discussed in this chapter – namely, Unity, Equilibrium, Free Will, and Responsibility – summarize all the basic aspects of these relationships. A central feature of these axioms is that they highlight the different, though mutually consistent, ways of establishing man's three-pronged relationship; they also point out the significance of this relationship for man's economic and social behaviour. In this, as in other respects, Islam insists on a balance (*mizan*) in personal attitudes and social behaviour. Thus, human freedom is not allowed to degenerate into unlimited licence for the exercise of private property rights; nor is social responsibility designed as a vehicle for human bondage. Also, man is denied the convenient constraint of predestination by making him responsible for his actions. Thus, here we have the terms of reference of a *consequence-sensitive* Islamic ethics, whereby man is committed to the welfare of the society – in particular to the amelioration of the lot of its least-privileged members. Another way of looking at the matter is that man is committed to the preservation of his own freedom *and* that of others in society. The job of the social scientist, therefore, is to establish a procedure for ascertaining an ethical perspective, in man's economic activities. We turn to this task in the next chapter.

NOTES

1 The ensuing discussion draws selectively on Naqvi (1981a) and (1981b).
2 The Quranic technique in this connection is that when it speaks of God Himself, it puts utmost emphasis on His omnipotence: 'Verily God does as He pleases' (22:14) 'God creates whatsoever He pleases' (24:45); 'He is witness over all things' (41:53) On the other hand, when the Quran talks about man's freedom and responsibility, it

gives him freedom of action: 'Every soul is entangled in what it does' (74:58); 'Say: O men, the truth has come to you from you Lord, so he who follows the right path does so for himself, and he who goes astray errs against himself, and I am not a guardian over you' (10:108).
3 Eaton (1987) remarks, 'except in rare cases, [man's] Vicegerency is no more than a virtuality yet to be realized'.
4 The distinction between the individual man and the collective man has been noted by Schuon (1963, pp. 26–27). See also Ahmad (1976, Ch.1), and Boisard (1987, pp. 99–111).
5 In the Marxian perspective, in a capitalist system 'the producer becomes alienated from his product through the mechanism of exchange, which makes the destination of his product a matter of indifference to him' [Caterphores (1990)].
6 There has been an intense debate among different schools of thought about the relative importance of each of the axioms noted in the text. With the beginning of theological formalization in Islam from the second half of the Second Century (A.H.), *Jabriya*, being the true sons of the fatalist Arabs, were the first to speak on this issue, and took the position of absolute power of God and predestination of human affairs, thus absolving man of all moral and ethical responsibilities. In reaction to the *Jabriya* school, the pietistic school of *Qadariya* and the rationalist school of the *Mu'tazila* (2nd to 4th Century), though not ignoring the omnipotence of God, put emphasis on man's freedom of will and his being responsible for his actions. Excessive emphasis on rationalism by the *Mu'tazila*, however, caused a severe reaction among the orthodox circles and Abu'l Hasan al Ash'ari (d. 330 A.H./942 A.D.) formulated his own theory of God's absolute omnipotence in relation to man's endeavour. However, even the Ash'arites could not absolve man of his responsibilities and had to propound their doctrine of 'acquisition' (*Kasb*). According to this doctrine, all acts are created by God, but it is the will of man who acquires them through his intention to act. Since the 5th Century (A.H.), the Asharite theology has remained the official creed of Islam. However, beginning with the 13th Century (A.H.) (19th Century, A.D.), there have been some serious reactions against the Ash'arite literalism, and there has been a revival of the Mu'tazilite rational approach led by such scholars as Shaykh Mohammad 'Abduh of Egypt, Zia Gökalp of Turkey, and Gamal al-Din al-Afghani, Sir Sayyid Ahmed Khan, Allama Muhammad Iqbal, and Sayyid Ameer Ali of India-Pakistan.

In the final analysis, we can say that, notwithstanding the differences of emphasis, there has been a tacit agreement among theologians that man is responsible for his acts, and that God, by His very nature, is just in deciding man's fate according to his deeds. Concomitantly, therefore, man must have freedom of will in shaping his destiny. This note is based on Jafri (1988). For details, see Watt (1948); Boer (1970); Shahrastani (1978); Al-Ash'ari (1929); Gibb and Kramers (1961); Wensinck (1932). By far the best analytical account is given by Fazlur Rahman (1968). For modern interpretations, see Iqbal (1986); Ameer Ali (1922); and 'Abduh (1908).

7 However, the theomorphism of man does not purport to establish any commensurability between man and God. It is merely an assertion of the relativity of man in relation to God. But this relativity makes him 'the spokesman of creation, doubly representative; for if he represents God in the province of the world, he also represents the world before God' [Eaton (1987), p. 376].

8 This aspect of Unity is discussed in Nasr (1968, 1979). See also Qutb (1976) for the social implications of Unity.

9 For a full discussion of these ideas, see Nasr (1987).

10 Sadr (1982) has laid great emphasis on this aspect of societal transformation which begins with the individual and ends with the society.

11 To avoid confusion, the reader should note that the word 'Equilibrium' has been used in this book to convey the meanings of *al 'Adl* and *al Ihsan*. Sadr (1982) uses the term 'social balance' for *al 'Adl*; but his connotation applies more naturally to the related Quranic concept of *al-Mizan*.

12 For a detailed description of this concept, see Naqvi (1981a; 1981b); Naqvi et al. (1980) and Naqvi et al. (1984).

13 The Quran stipulates: 'In whose wealth a due share is included for the needy and those dispossessed' (70:24–25). Mawdudi (1976) remarks that this Quranic verse was revealed in Makka, where a Muslim society had not yet been established. Thus, according to him, the verse in the text clearly denotes 'that anyone who asks for help and anyone who is suffering from deprivation has a right to share in the property and wealth of a Muslim, irrespective of whether he belongs to this or that nation, to this or that country, to this or that race' (p. 19).

14 Indeed, at the theological level, the quality of Equilibrium *defines* Islam itself, which can also be seen as a Providential Synthesis of the Divine aspects of Mercy and Justice. See Schuon (1975).

15 As the Quran says, God 'created every thing and determined its exact measures' (25:2). A fine balancing of social forces is already prefigured in the Universe which is in a state of uninterrupted equilibrium: 'Neither can the sun overtake the moon, nor the night outpace the day: Each of them keeps coursing in its orbit' (36–40).

16 In a deeper sense, *Jihad* denotes waging a war against evil, both within and without ourselves.

17 Also note another contextual difference in the use of the term Equilibrium. In economics, one is normally satisfied with equilibrium solutions without enquiring about their normative contents. However, in the Islamic perspective, unethical optimal solutions are simply not admissible.

18 Thus, man has been advised to seek God's Mercy to help him 'see' the 'right path': 'Guide us (O Lord) to the path that is straight, the path of those You have blessed, not to those who have earned Your anger, nor those who have gone astray' (1:5, 6, 7).

THE ETHICAL FOUNDATIONS

19 The contents of footnote 3 of Chapter 7 are relevant here.
20 Schuon (1963) remarks: 'God alone is absolute freedom, but human freedom, despite its relativity (in the sense that it is relatively absolute), is nothing other than freedom any more than a feeble light is something other than light' (p. 14). But the point we make in the text is that, in practice, the Islamic light of freedom is not less feeble, nor any less potent, than the Kantian freedom; indeed, it is stronger and more translucent than any other light for reasons noted in the text.
21 See Ch. 4 of this book and footnote 17 for more details about the non-consequentialist view of moral rights.
22 There is an inherent difficulty in *translating* the timeless Divine message within the crucible of time-bound social institutions. The task of interpretation *adds* to this difficulty.
23 Many Islamicists have emphasized the centrality of the concept of responsibility. Iqbal (1986) sees responsibility as implied by the 'fact' that man is a trustee of a free personality. Shariati (1974) has defined it more explicitly. See also Ali (1922). But the discussion by these authors is somewhat one-sided, emphasizing responsibility more than freedom; which is *not* the Islamic intent. In contrast, Sadr (1982) gives an accurate account of the Islamic concept of responsibility.
24 For instance, as an economic concept, responsibility is not merely represented by the 'interdependence of individual welfare functions' – i.e., where the welfare of an individual is directly influenced by that of another – but goes much further. See chapters 6 and 7 of this book.
25 'Have you seen him who denies the Day of Judgement? It is he who pushes the orphan away, And does not induce others to feed the needy' (107:1–3). This verse makes clear that man should not only be doing good himself, but also should be urging others to do the same.
26 These matters are discussed in more detail in Naqvi (1981b).
27 I owe this clarification to Khurshid Ahmed's 'Foreword' to my book (1981a). He suggests that the distinction between *Fard 'ala al 'ain* (individual responsibility that is non-transferable) and *Fard 'ala al Kifayah* (collective responsibility dischargeable by a few) must be kept in view in explaining the Islamic concept of responsibility.

Part II

A MODEL OF ISLAMIC ETHICAL AXIOMS

4

THE FRAMING OF AXIOMS OF ISLAMIC ETHICS

We need to identify Islamic ethical postulates of sufficient generality to deduce the principles of Islamic economics. As asserted in the previous chapter, Islamic ethics is represented by a set of axioms containing four elements – namely, Unity, Equilibrium, Free Will, and Responsibility. We now take the next logical step to show that this set possesses all the characteristics of a 'spanning set' – i.e., one that can serve, in the present context, as a 'basis' for deducing economic statements.[1] But to qualify as a basis, the set of ethical principles must adequately summarize Islam's ethical philosophy. This does not mean that the set includes *all aspects* of Islamic ethics, but that it includes *all those aspects* which are relevant for deducing the rules of economic behaviour. However, with respect to such aspects, the set must be comprehensive.

RELIGION AS A SOURCE OF ETHICAL AXIOMS

It may be useful to note at the very outset that, unlike a Western social philosopher for whom religion is forbidden territory, for a Muslim thinker in search of an appropiate ethical basis, it (religion) is *not* forbidden territory.[2] For him the Quran and the *Sunnah* of the Prophet are the primary sources of Islamic ethics, which can be used to deduce general principles of economic behaviour for the simple reason that economic agents *believe* in it. Fortunately, such a belief is not a prescription for maintaining an unjust *status quo*, because Islam does not subscribe to any unalterable institutional hierarchy, nor does it subscribe to any non-consequentialist view of moral rights;[3] instead, it helps cultivate, at the social level, a keen sensitivity to the exercise of the individual's moral rights, and recommends corrective action when such consequences are socially (and morally) unacceptable.

There is also the important methodological question about the *feasibility* of the research programme of Islamic economics – of trying to discover areas where economic behaviour is derivable from ethical criteria. If by the feasibility of the enterprise is meant its capacity to achieve its objectives, then the proof of the pudding is in the eating. However, if the feasibility of the research programme is to be decided in *advance* by reference to the scientific character of the enterprise, then the danger for Islamic economics to fail the test is no greater than what mainstream economics has always faced! After all, the most successful part of economics – i.e., the theory of value – has been axiomatized and deduced logically from a number of basic postulates, which are essentially *non-verifiable*.[4] Indeed, most positive economics is based on either mere platitudes (e.g., individuals tend to choose that option which they prefer most), or it relies on sheer simplifications (e.g., individuals possess perfect information). But nobody will think of discarding all economics on these grounds, certainly not the economists whose bread and butter is linked with the prosperity of their science. Thus, the feasibility of the research programme need not be doubted, even if it can be shown that the basic ethical postulates of Islamic economics are essentially *non-verifiable*. But there is every reason for a Muslim economist to feel fortified on this account, because the ethical postulates of Islamic economics are essentially verifiable as they form an integral part of the beliefs held by the Muslims, whose actual behaviour must also reflect them. (See Chapter 2).

THE CHARACTERISTICS OF THE SYSTEM OF ETHICAL AXIOMS

We now take the first logical step in our enquiry into the foundations of Islamic economics. It is to construct a minimal non-trivial set of ethical axioms, in the sense that there is no set contained in or subsumed by it which is non-trivial.[5] The set of ethical axioms must also be comprehensive to serve as an adequate basis for generating a large enough number of economic statements; if this is not so, then for every axiom in the set there will exist another axiom outside it to serve the same purpose.

A set of ethical axioms possessing the above-mentioned attributes must satisfy five properties in order to serve as a basis – i.e., to be able to generate economic statements of sufficient generality.[6] First, the set should be an *adequate* and a *legitimate* representation of Islam's ethical views. This property ensures that of the *infinite number of axioms co-existing with the finite set stipulated*, only those which are legitimate qualify to be in the set – i.e., they derive from the Quran and the *Sunnah*. This requirement precludes subjective arbitrariness in the choice of ethical axioms.

Second, the collection of axioms must be a spanning set; it should form a 'basis'. According to this requirement, such a set cannot be reduced any further in any non-trivial sense because it is large enough to generate all else. In the present case, it means generating a significant number of economic statements. The basis need not be unique, as there could exist an infinite number of bases;[7] but the presumption is that the basis actually chosen would be the most 'efficient' in the sense just specified.

The third property relates to the *independence* of the set. This property is vital for the validity of the axiom system. The independence of a mathematical axiom system is checked by establishing the independence of its elements from each other, which is proved by showing that no element (i.e., axiom) in the set is deducible from any other element of the set.[8] If, after performing such an experiment, each element is shown to be independent, then the set containing such elements will also be independent.

The fourth property of the set is that all its elements must be *consistent* with each other.[9] A proof of this is given in the literature by showing that none of the elements in the set is deducible in a manner that one can be the negation of the other. In other words, the truth and the falsity of the same assertion in the set cannot be deduced simultaneously. The consistency test can also be applied in a more heuristic sense; that the truth of one axiom should not belie the truth of another axiom in the set, and that each of the axioms in the set must point to a common truth about the system as a whole. Specifically, for the purposes of this study, we should check that when the axiom system is oriented towards the Islamic ethical value perspective, none of the elements should contradict it.

The fifth property of the set relates to its *predictive* power, that it is capable of generating a series of singular statements from the set of axioms taken as a basis.[10] In general, the expectation is that these singular statements are empirically verifiable. In the present context, our aim is to generate, from the set of ethical axioms noted above, a number of (meaningful) statements relevant to Islamic economics.

Another property, pointed out by Popper (1980), is that the axiom system should be *sufficient* to deduce all the basic statements; and that it is also *necessary* to exclude the presence of any superfluous assumptions.

In addition to the satisfaction of these formal properties of ethical axioms, we should seek, in the words of Weber (1949), 'an understanding' of the social phenomenon under enquiry. This should especially be a characteristic of the inquiry in Islamic economics, where we wish to study specific phenomena in detail and for their own sake instead of looking at them only as special aspects of some general theories. Once again, this property can be used in a heuristic way to see whether or not a certain set of ethical axioms gives us an insight into the economics of Muslim society.

THE 'EFFICIENCY' OF THE ISLAMIC ETHICAL AXIOM SYSTEM

It has been asserted in Chapter 3 that Islam's ethical philosophy is representable by a set of only four axioms – namely, Unity, Equilibrium, Free Will, and Responsibility. As noted above, this set is not necessarily unique in the sense of being the only one possible to make valid generalizations about the Islamic economic system; but we do assert that for the present purpose this is the most *efficient* possible set. That it is *a* (not *the*) spanning set can be established by showing that the postulated ethical axiom system satisfies all the axiomatic properties noted in the preceding section: that it is the minimal non-trivial set; that it is consistent; that all elements of the set are independent; and that it possesses predictive power. Furthermore, we show that this is an efficient set because it is both necessary and sufficient to generate all the relevant economic statements; and also that it provides a deeper understanding of the economic phenomenon in the Islamic society than is otherwise possible.

Thus far, we have stated that the proposed set of ethical axioms is non-trivial; that it is a non-null set containing four elements. It is also a minimal set in the sense of forming a basis. To see this, let us drop from the set one or more of the elements of the set and see whether it still retains the characteristics of a spanning set – whether, in a loose sense, it still contains the same amount of information about the Islamic economic system.[11] For instance, one can argue that Unity and Equilibrium give the same information since both these are the attributes of God Himself – Who is the one and the only one (*al-Wahid*), and Who is also the ultimate in 'justice' (*al 'Adil*). Similarly, one may assert that Responsibility may be seen as implied by Free Will; hence the set of axioms should contain only two elements, Unity and Free Will, or Unity and Responsibility; but not all of them. Pursuing this line of argument, one can assert that the Unity axiom is really the only independent element in the set, all the rest being redundant.

Indeed, some Muslim scholars have employed the concept of Unity alone to deduce all basic principles of Islamic economics, including the concept of social justice in Islam. The argument furthered is that since all else in the world is a reflection of God, Who is Unity, all desirable properties of the social and economic universe must be deducible from the same source.[13]

However, this line of argument is erroneous because God has many attributes which, independent of each other, make explicit one or another of His qualities. Thus, logically, Equilibrium is not deducible from Unity. As pointed out in the preceding chapter, while Unity is the vertical dimension of Islam, Equilibrium is its horizontal dimension, even though both these dimensions are prefigured in God's Nature. In other words, Unity does not automatically make explicit the divine quality of Equilibrium. Hence, the concept of Equilibrium must be introduced to make clear the Islamic perspective, according to which God is essentially *al 'Adil*. Similarly, it can be shown that the remaining two axioms – i.e., Free Will and Responsibility – are also essential elements of the set as one does not necessarily imply the other. For instance, Free Will can as much lead to anarchy as to social harmony. Also, Responsibility, if pushed too far, can be destructive of man's freedom and, thus, be a source of *Zulm* (disequilibrium) instead of being a factor maximizing social welfare. Thus, each of the four elements of the set is required in order to decide in a specific societal context the question of establishing a proportion and a balance between them. In other words, none of the elements of the set is redundant. Therefore, this set forms a basis.

That the set is consistent can be established by showing that it is not possible to draw just any conclusions from it, so that the truth of one axiom is in no way contradicted by any of the other axioms in the set. All four axioms in the set highlight some essential aspects of the Islamic ethical philosophy, which aims at producing a harmonious and just socio-economic ordering of free men, who are committed not only to maximizing their own welfare but also the welfare of others in the society; and who insist not only on securing increments in their material welfare but also on enhancing their spiritual welfare. As pointed out above, this cannot happen if Free Will, so to speak, is allowed a free hand; or if men are saddled only with Responsibility towards others, without enough opportunities for their personal welfare. Thus, both Free Will and Responsibility are needed in the set to highlight vital aspects of Islam's ethical philosophy. It will also not be morally right if, wrongly referring to the Unity axiom, all men are treated equally, without regard to the differences in their social stations, and measured by their current income levels or their initial wealth holdings. The Equilibrium axiom will recognize such differences and aim at a just redistribution of income and wealth. It also follows that both Unity and Equilibrium are needed in the set. In this way, it can also be shown that each element in the set 'matters' – i.e., the elements in the set are consistent with each other, so that none of the elements in the basis can be expressed in terms of any other element in the set.

The *independence* of the set can be proved also by demonstrating that none of the elements of the set is deducible from the rest. This property should be apparent also from the discussion in the preceding paragraph and needs no further comment. That the set of axioms also possesses enough 'predictive power' can be seen by checking that it offers both the *necessary* and *sufficient* conditions to generate (singular) statements about the Islamic economic system – i.e., the Islamic economic system implies the postulated set of axioms and these axioms imply an Islamic economic system. The *necessary* part of this statement can be proved by showing that the set of axioms is independent. Its *sufficiency* follows from the demonstration, which is the main burden of this book, that all the basic principles of an Islamic economy can be derived from the set of axioms plus a few additional *hypotheses*.[13] This is what we shall show in the rest of the book. Another way of looking at the matter is to convert the 'if and only' condition into two 'if' parts: namely, the set of ethical axioms implies the existence of an Islamic economy; and the Islamic economy implies the set. The truth of these assertions should be transparent if it is kept in mind that both the Islamic economic system and the ethical axiom system are based on the Quran and the *Sunnah*. They must, therefore, imply each other.

Finally, it can be shown easily that the ethical axiom system adds to our understanding about the nature of the Islamic ethical system. We have already shown that the set of axioms is comprehensive, and is a minimal non-trivial set; it possesses all the standard properties of a typical axiom system. This shows, among other things, that the Islamic ethical system is 'universally' valid. Furthermore, this set not only describes Islamic ethics but can also be used as a 'basis' for generating valid statements of Islamic economics, an assertion which should clarify the normative character of Islamic economics.

TOWARDS A NORMATIVE ISLAMIC ECONOMICS

As noted in Chapter 2, *Islamic economics* addresses both the *is* questions and the *ought* questions. For instance, once the adverse consequences of a certain action become obvious – e.g., the exercise of private property rights by one economic agent hurts the interests of others in the society – Islam makes it morally mandatory on the state to take corrective action. Thus, there is no such thing as 'neutrality' when confronted with making a choice between a just situation and an unjust situation. In other words, Islam insists not only on efficient solutions but also on just solutions.[14]

The discussion thus far shows that the procedure of deducing economic statements from ethical axioms is a scientifically correct procedure; and that it is also capable of yielding a series of testable hypotheses about an Islamic economy. Above all, Islamic economics leads us to address *new* issues, the most important of which is to *synthesize ethics and economics within a single framework*. It also suggests a framework for analysing these issues adequately.[15]

Once the importance of ethical considerations is fully grasped, it becomes obvious that Robbins's (1932) famous definition of economics 'as the science which studies human behaviour as a relationship between ends and scarce means which have alternative uses' appears to be unduly restrictive. This is because by firmly excluding ethics as irrelevant to making valid economic statements, it confines economics to studying only the conflict situations, the situations which are by their very nature competitive.[16] Fortunately, the real world is richer than that. Repeated simulation studies show that many significant situations marked by an insistence of each player to care *only* for his own welfare – illustrated graphically by the oft-quoted Prisoner's Dilemma case – can end up being to everyone's disadvantage [Simon (1983)]. In all such cases, cooperative strategies yield a superior collective outcome. Indeed, a little reflection should show that it is more *economical* to relate Robbins's scarce means to his multiple ends if each economic agent does not always insist *only* on his own self-interest, but also thinks about the welfare of others. In such a scenario, significant amounts of real resources will be released *voluntarily* from the pursuit of personal greed for the greater good of the society.

Islamic economics is also normative in the sense of being *consequence-sensitive*. It not only discusses the questions of property rights, but also insists on the state to take corrective action if the exercise of (private) property rights has adverse social consequences. The Islamic morality emphasizes both the individual's innate freedom *and* his social responsibility in the same breath. This insistence on consequence-sensitivity immediately implies that Islamic economics will have no use for those decision rules – e.g., Pareto-optimality – which approve of the *status quo* even if it be an undesirable social state for the poor. By the same token, Islam would also reject those moral right theories which are strictly procedural and consequence-insensitive – e.g., Nozick's entitlements theory.[17] Instead, it insists on the 'rights' of the poor in the wealth of the rich, and to prescribe (legislative) action in case such rights are not enjoyed by the poor in the due course.

It should be noted that while Islamic economics is consequentialist, it is not necessarily 'welfarist' – that Islam does not measure welfare by the metric of utility alone.[18] This is because by admitting *only* utility information, and by neglecting all other kinds of information about a person – e.g., his income, his ownership of certain 'commodities', etc. – one is totally incapacitated to distinguish between the rich and the poor; because while the rich may be the hard-to-please type of persons, as they usually are, the poor may be contented even with small increments in their happiness. That being the case, an exclusively utilitarian measure of social welfare may give *more* income to the *rich* and *less* income to the *poor*. Such a perverse result would be contrary to Islam's ethical philosophy.

Such a procedure of going from ethics to economics should cause no qualms to the scientist's conscience because he always uses a pre-assigned value system as a reference point for making scientific statements. Indeed, scientific behaviour, in general, is motivated by a goal and a set of values. This is all the more true of economic behaviour. Thus, the search for value/ethics-free decision rules is both pointless and counter-productive even from a purely scientific point of view.[19] Such statements involve a logical fallacy of calling value-free and scientific (or objective) a statement about which there exists some kind of a consensus. For instance, if Pareto-optimality implies a vote for the *status quo*, this does not mean that the principle is value-free; in fact, it implies a value judgement *against* social change! Fortunately, hard-core economic theory is now no longer bound by Robbins's irrevocable vow to keep economics free of value judgements.[20]

Following Arrow's influential work (1951), there is now an impressive body of literature in public-choice theory which shows how alternative judgements can be expressed in an axiomatic form and evaluated in terms of their logical implications.[21] Thus, Harsanyi's equi-probability model is based on the observation that 'each individual . . . has an equal probability of being any other in the society.' (Mueller, 1979, p. 251). The key insight of the model is that individuals are motivated by both personal *and* moral reasons. Similarly, in the Rawlsian model, free and equal persons typically make a mental experiment to take impartial decisions to choose fair(er) institutions. The aim is to evaluate the goodness of a state of affairs by reference to the welfare of the worst-off individuals in the society. And there are many other such decision rules – e.g., those employing universally accepted principles of impartiality, universality, impersonality – which take account of the ethical norms in the society.[22]

Where Islamic (normative) economics differs from the public-choice theory is that the latter does not accept religion as the place to find moral principles;[23] by contrast, for the former, religion is *the* natural place to find the basic moral principles.

SUMMARY

In this and the previous chapters we have tried to establish that the proposed ethical axiom system is an adequate representation of Islam's ethical point of view, and that it is also the proper analytical tool to explore the nature of Islamic economics. The most attractive feature of this framework is that it consists of a minimal number of elements – Unity, Equilibrium, Free Will, and Responsibility. *Nothing more and nothing less*. Anything less will make the set an inadequate tool of analysis; while adding anything more to the set will be a redundant step – because each such addition to the set can be shown as prefigured in or implied by the spanning set. This set of ethical values also possesses all the major characteristics of a logically sound axiom system: it is minimal, consistent, and independent; it can make meaningful predictions about the Islamic economy; it is both necessary and sufficient; and it adds to our understanding of the Islamic economic universe. We also show that this set of axioms captures the central message of Islamic social philosophy – namely, the rejection of an unjust *status quo* and a call for social change where it is needed.

The Muslims look to their religion for guidance in their daily lives. As shown in Chapter 2, it is unsatisfactory to study the behaviour of such economic agents in isolation from the moral principles in which they believe. The strength of the analytical procedure outlined in the present chapter is the use of ethical beliefs in a typical Muslim society as a basis for deriving logically valid principles of 'economic' behaviour. Such a demonstration adds to our knowledge by pointing out the importance of ethico-religious considerations for economics, both at the philosophical and the empirical levels.

NOTES

1. This procedure also implies that to serve as a 'basis', the axioms of Islamic ethics should be determined independently instead of being made contingent to the acceptance of specific (Islamic) policy options. The importance of this implication will become clear when we come to discuss specific policy options in Chapters 10 and 11.
2. For instance, Rawls (1985) does not consider religious values as relevant for judging the justness of a certain social order partly because such an order is often mistaken for 'a fixed natural order' (p. 231).
3. For the non-consequentialist view of moral rights, see Nozick (1974).
4. For instance, Machlup (1956) argues that the profit-maximization postulate, in the sense of a consistent profit-maximizing conduct on the part of firms, cannot be verified to be true; only the logical *outcome* of such a postulate *may* be verifiable. To give another example, note that the same would be true of the various postulates of the Arrow-Debreu micro-economics.
5. That it needs to be a minimal non-trivial set should also be clear, because a trivial minimal set would be a null set – i.e., having zero as its only element. And such a non-trivial set should be minimal because, otherwise, it could not serve as a 'basis' in the mathematical sense.
6. These general requirements must be satisfied by *all* logical axiom systems. For an excellent discussion of these matters, see Novikov (1964).
7. See Hadley (1964, pp. 39–45) for a full discussion of this point. This mathematical property relates to the Euclidean space; but, to a lesser extent, it is also applicable to the social space, where there is less room for forming meaningful combinations of axioms.
8. Popper (1980) points out that a statement qualifies as an axiom only if it is not deducible from any other element in the axiom system.
9. Popper (1980) regards the consistency requirement to be the most basic because an inconsistent (self-contradictory) system is 'uninformative', i.e., it can be made to yield just any statement we please.
10. For a detailed discussion of the process of making predictions from axiom systems, see Popper (1980).
11. This question entails asking two connected questions. Is there a smaller set? And is there a bigger set? In the text, we discuss the first question and get a negative answer. But the reasons for a negative answer to the second question as well are easy to understand. For instance, some Muslim economists assert that the Islamic concept of *Khalifa* (vicegerent) should also be included in the set. (See Ahmed's 'Foreword' to Naqvi, 1981). But the falsity of this assertion can be established quickly by reference to the fact that the Free Will axiom gives the same information – that man is God's vicegerent on earth – *plus* the additional point that man is born with the freedom to make his own choices. Thus, the replacement of Free Will by *Khalifa* in the set will give either the same amount of

information or less; also the co-existence of both the axioms in the set will make the set non-basic – i.e., it will no longer be a minimal set.
12. See, Qutb (1976), and Sulaiman (1979) for this line of argument.
13. Some of these hypotheses are listed in Chapter 4.
14. A consequence of this position is that not all of the Pareto-optimal solutions will be acceptable; but only those which also satisfy certain minimum ethical requirements from the Islamic point of view.
15. In this sense, Islamic economics may be considered as a scientific research programme [Lakatos (1970)].
16. Robbins's definition excludes not only ethics but a lot more. As Hausman (1984) points out, by *defining* economics as a neoclassical theory, this definition also excludes from its purview things like Keynesian economics!
17. Nozick (1974) holds a strictly procedural view of moral rights and cautions against 'patterning' income distribution because 'from the point of view of [his] entitlement theory, redistribution is a serious matter; indeed, involving as it does the violation of people's rights.' (p. 168). But such a view would be unacceptable from an Islamic point of view. Thus, as Sadr (1982) and Taleghani (1982) point out, Islam would abolish morally unjust and economically counter-productive (legal) feudal systems, which accord priority to the rights of non-cultivators over the rights of cultivators.
18. Islam would also not accept the 'sum-ranking' criterion of Benthamite utilitarianism, whereby the utility information about a specific social state is evaluated exclusively in terms of the sum total of utilities. See Sen (1987) for a factorization of the utilitarian philosophy into 'welfarism', 'sum-ranking', and 'consequentialism'.
19. A vast literature discussing the pros and cons of this point of view has developed under the title of Social Choice Theory. See Sen (1987) for a review of the relevant literature.
20. Harsanyi (1991) concludes: 'There was a time when many economists [led by Robbins] wanted to ensure the objectivity of economic analysis by excluding value judgements, and even the study of value judgements, from economic ... Luckily, they have not succeeded; and we know now that economics would have been that much poorer if they had.' p. 704.
21. See Sen (1987) and Naqvi (1993) for further discussion regarding this issue.
22. For a review of such theories, see Naqvi (1993).
23. For instance, the Rawlsian conception of 'justice as fairness', which in some respects is relevant for Islamic economics, does *not* recognize religious values as helpful in judging the justness of a given social order. See Rawls (1985).

5
THE RULES OF ECONOMIC BEHAVIOUR IN AN ISLAMIC ECONOMY

The focus of the analysis presented so far has been on determining a set of ethical postulates from which a sufficiently large number of valid statements about an Islamic economy can be deduced. Thus, we have identified a set of axioms which adequately summarize Islam's ethical stance. The stage is now set to deduce from these a few key propositions (statements) of Islamic economics. It needs to be reiterated that the use of deductive logic to derive rules of economic behaviour in an Islamic economy does not make empirical reasoning redundant. Far from that; all that is being done is to derive empirically *verifiable* hypotheses about an essentially normative Islamic economics. To this end, as noted in Chapter 2, the concept of a Muslim society has been used to serve as a real-life counterpart of an (idealized) Islamic society. This concept has also been used to make the choice of the set of axioms look plausible on empirical grounds – even though, from a methodological point of view, this step is seldom taken, except by the 'ultra-empiricists'.

FROM AXIOMS TO RULES OF ECONOMIC BEHAVIOUR

The set of axioms identified in the preceding chapters – namely, Unity, Equilibrium, Free Will, and Responsibility – provide a basis for deducing rules of economic behaviour about an Islamic economy. However, going from the former to the latter involves taking two more analytical steps. First, as discussed at some length in Chapter 2, we should make sure that the rules of economic behaviour, deduced from the ethical postulates, do have a *chance* – even an outside chance – of being 'observed' in the real world. Specifically, the rules of economic behaviour in an Islamic economy must have some relation, however tenuous, with actual behaviour in a typical Muslim society. Second, we also need to 'add on' a few additional *hypotheses* to make the economic implications of the ethical axioms clearer.

It may be useful to clarify both these points at this stage, even at the cost of some repetition.

(a) In a sense, in the eyes of a representative Muslim, the ethical axioms discussed in Chapters 3 and 4 are of the nature of 'synthetic truths' about the real world – i.e., those which can be known *a priori* without any recourse to a confirmation through sensory experience. One is fortified in such a belief by the fact that these axioms are based on the Quran and the *Sunnah*. Having assured ourselves about the legitimacy of the Islamic ethical axioms noted above as a spanning set (of the basic postulates), the next logical step is to deduce a set of *empirically verifiable* economic propositions.

However, as noted in Chapter 2, while these axioms are regarded as synthetic truths in the world of Islam, the possibility of a sensory confirmation of the ethical postulates – even only of the fleeting shadows of these in the real world – is a definite advantage; however tentative may be the nature and scope of such a confirmation. Such a possibility is opened up by the fact that the (theological, metaphysical) belief in the Divine Presence is widely held without question by the representative Muslim; and that this belief significantly affects his social and economic behaviour. Not only that; the average Muslim takes his beliefs seriously in his day-to-day social and economic conduct. And this is what differentiates a *Muslim* society from any other society.[1] It also follows that rules of economic behaviour derived from such beliefs will differ from those held in other cultures significantly enough to warrant a different treatment.

(b) The second logical step in going from ethical axioms to Islamic economics is to add on to these axioms a few supporting *hypotheses* – indeed, *any* number of them, depending on what our analytical requirements are. The fulfilment of these hypotheses, on the one hand, 'brings down' the axioms to the economic sub-space and makes its economic meanings and implications more transparent; while, on the other hand, it broadens the list of valid conclusions drawn directly (and explicitly) from the axioms.

For our purposes, we postulate four such hypotheses.

(i) Economic activity is indissolubly linked with man's ethical environment.

(ii) Economic policy should aim at a 'just' balance among the basic production, consumption, and distribution relations, with an ample provision made for those members of the society who cannot, even if they want to, participate in the economic life of the community.

(iii) Income and wealth should be redistributed when the existing pattern of distribution is not 'just' from the Islamic point of view.

(iv) Within the framework of a set of ground rules, individual (economic) freedom should be guaranteed; but the state should be allowed to regulate it in cases where the exercise of individual freedom becomes inconsistent with social welfare.

This chapter spells out the logical consequences of ethical axioms *plus* these hypotheses on the behaviour of economic agents in an Islamic economy.

RATIONAL BEHAVIOUR AND ETHICAL ENVIRONMENT

(i) Ethics and Rational Behaviour

The concept of rationality in economics, also equated with self-interest maximization behaviour, is meant to simulate the actual behaviour of economic agents. This simplification, central to neoclassical economics, ensures the positivity of economics by keeping ethics out in the cold. It is for this reason that all ethical behaviour, which is not necessarily in keeping with self-interest maximization, is termed irrational. But this line of reasoning is at fault on several grounds.[2] First, we note that from the Islamic point of view this is an unacceptable proposition *even as a simplification*. This is because rationality in Islam is *defined* in a manner that ethical imperatives and economic exigencies get intermingled both at the philosophical level and the social level.

Second, as noted earlier in Chapter 2, the belief in the Divine Presence impels a representative Muslim to act out of ethical compulsions. Such a belief is mainly responsible for a pattern of spending even on the part of the individuals who are not particularly religious that cannot be explained otherwise. Associated with this belief is the thought of the Hereafter which influences economic behaviour. With such a perception, rational behaviour will have to be defined broadly enough to include the reward of the good deeds in the Hereafter.[3]

Third, the Responsibility axiom, which makes it morally *binding* on the individual to act for the welfare of the society *as well*, also dampens relentless self-interest maximization. It does so by excluding the assumption of the independence of utility functions, made routinely in positive economics, even as a 'stylized' fact of life in the Islamic society. In the Islamic belief 'Allah's is the heritage of the heavens and the earth' (3:180). That being the case, it is *rational* to act as a trustee in deference to the Quranic injunction: 'and spend of that whereof He hath made you trustees' (57:7).

(ii) The 'Priority' of Individual Liberty

The problem of priority – of ordering different indices of personal and social well-being – has to be faced both at the theoretical and the practical levels. In particular, the question of the place of individual liberty in the scale of social values must be faced. As noted above, Islam accepts individual freedom as an absolute value (Free Will axiom), but also puts limits on it only when the exercise of personal freedom becomes obviously inconsistent with social well-being (Responsibility axiom).

To see the Islamic point of view more clearly, let us consider two polar cases. Thus, one could make individual freedom to be entirely subservient to social well-being – the so-called 'dictatorship solution'. The state, then, becomes the conscience of the society, acting on behalf of the individuals. Or one could go to the other extreme and accord a priority, *à la* Rawls (1971), to individual liberty over all else. In the same vein, according to the non-consequentialist moral-rights approach to the problem, what must not be tampered with by social legislation is the individual's right to liberty, his entitlement to the ownership of property, his freedom to use the fruits of the exercise of such rights in the way that he wants, and his option to exchange them in the manner that he wishes, and bequeath to whomsoever he desires [Nozick (1974)]. According to this extremist formulation, the free and unhindered exercise of individual moral rights can *legitimately* coexist with extreme poverty, starvation, and famine.

In the light of the preceding discussion it should be obvious that such extremist formulations will *not* pass the test of Islamic morality. As noted below, the dictatorship solution is definitely repugnant to the Islamic commitment to human freedom. But the extremist libertarian views also would not be acceptable to Islam. This is because, paying due regard to the Equilibrium axiom, Islam emphasizes the quality of *distributive justice*, thus rejecting Benthamite utilitarianism and Nozickian non-consequentialism, as well as the Rawlsian emphasis on *individual liberty to the exclusion of all else*. This is because, as noted previously in this book, Islam accords a central importance to the welfare of the least-privileged in the society – even if that involves making suitable adjustments in the individual's liberty with respect to the exercise of the private ownership rights. Then, as noted above, an individual is not an absolute owner of his property but a trustee, and is not free to do *whatever* he likes to do with his wealth. For instance, ownership rights cease on the death of an individual so that the disposal of property is regulated by the laws of inheritance rather than by his whims.

Now, it may be asserted that there is a contradiction in all this; the Equilibrium and Responsibility axioms contradict the Free Will axiom. But a moment's reflection should show that once the 'dictatorship solution' is excluded from consideration, there is no real contradiction in simultaneously holding a position that *an* individual is free and that all individuals are free. To maintain that only one of these positions can be held is really to trivialize the problem of devising a set of rules which may ensure a peaceful social *co-existence* in a civilized society.

(iii) Ethics and Consumer Behaviour

The neoclassical economic theory of the Walrasian vintage firmly excludes the effect of ethical factors on the decision-making process of the consumers (and the producers).[4] Indeed, ever since Adam Smith pronounced his verdict divorcing economics from ethics, most authoritative renditions of neoclassical economics equate rational behaviour with self-interest behaviour.[5] Even stronger is the implication that self-interest behaviour is rational behaviour; so that any activity other than maximizing self-interest is treated as irrational. Thus, for instance, a consumer's behaviour is rational if he ranks states of the economy with respect to his *own* commodity bundles. This is the *selfishness-of-preferences* assumption, which is absolutely fundamental to the modern theory of value.[6]

Now selfishness will be taken into account as a fact of life even in Islamic economics; but it cannot be retained as a fundamental axiom in the *models* of a Muslim society – that is, in the *Islamic* society – since it insists on a confluence of the economic and ethical behaviours of man. We will return to this question in the next section, but let us note here a few fundamental amendments that will have to be made in the theory of consumer behaviour in such a society.

Firstly, the utility function of the consumer will be subject (i) to a feasibility constraint, i.e., whether the commodity bundle is producible; and (ii) to an additional *allowability constraint*, according to which certain commodities, the consumption of which has been prohibited – i.e., set equal to zero, are 'bads'. The introduction of these constraints will have certain definite consequences for Islamic economics. The 'free-disposal' assumption routinely made in neoclassical economics can't be made in Islamic economics; so that the commodity space will be 'defined' differently. In the case of 'bads' – e.g., alcohol – for which complete prohibition has been prescribed, this cost will be large enough to offset any economic gains flowing from this source. Hence, the consumption, production, and distribution of such goods will also be zero. On the other hand, the production of goods which increase public welfare as well – i.e., those which generate some external economies – may still be undertaken by the individual, though not optimally. This is because while ethical considerations may moderate somewhat the dictates of profit maximization, it will not be reasonable to assume that unaltruistic behaviour will disappear in an Islamic economy. Indeed, Islam does not envisage such an event. Thus, in all cases where strong external economies are present – e.g., education, health, etc. – state intervention will be required in an Islamic economy.

Secondly, in the commodity space emerging from this additional constraint, the consumption of the commodities actually produced will not be 'insatiable'. Thus, the utility-maximizing consumption basket will be differently 'loaded' in an Islamic economy. This also implies that even the profit-maximizing behaviour will lead economic agents to produce just such a consumption basket. But more on it later.

Thirdly, assigning positive values to ethical considerations will change the 'character' of competitive equilibrium, since the 'contents' of the efficiency locus will be different in this case. This is because (a) the commodity mix will be different in an Islamic economy, with a substantial increase in the share of wage goods; and (b) the social welfare function in the Islamic society, in all probability, will select a different point on the efficiency locus.

Fourthly, because of the ethical restrictions imposed on the utility-maximizing behaviour, the usual assumption made in the neoclassical theory about the independence of the consumption and production behaviours will also not hold in the revised theory of consumer behaviour. This is because in such a world an economic agent can no longer remain completely 'selfish' in his consumption behaviour; nor can he produce independently of what others are producing. In other words, *the inter-dependence of the utility functions and the production functions must be explicitly taken into account.*

Fifthly, there is a basic problem with taking self-interest maximization as a sole indicator of rationality. Once ethical considerations are taken into account, such a narrow characterization of rationality becomes untenable.[7] Recognizing that each man is both an individual person and a collective person,[8] it becomes quite natural for him to act rationally and yet be *committed* to certain goals and ideals, especially those relating to raising the welfare of the poor. Thus, helping others (the poor and the needy) would be a rational act *because*: 'You will never come to piety unless you spend of things you love' (3:92). However, a preference for commitment does *not* mean that an Islamic economy will be characterized wholly, or even predominantly, by altruism; but only that such a preference is held out as an ideal to guide the individual out of excessive greed and selfishness.

Lastly, the preference for the act of giving to the least-priviledged in the society raises difficult problems for the neoclassical theory of consumer behaviour, which assumes that consumer preferences are 'continuous' – besides being complete, transitive, and reflexive. But, in the Islamic model of man, social preferences with respect to alternative states of the economy will not be 'continuous'; instead they will be 'lexicographic', which denotes discontinuous behaviour.[9]

(iii) Pareto-Optimality as a Social-Choice Rule?

One of the basic concepts of neoclassical economics, namely, the Pareto-optimality principle,[10] will be quite inadequate as a guide for Islamic economics. This is because this rule is empty of any ethical content, even though it is held by its proponents as both 'fair' and liberal – fair, because it reflects unanimity about the status quo;[11] liberal, because it (allegedly) preserves liberty. There is an extensive discussion in the literature showing the falsity of this line of reasoning [Sen (1983)]. We examine here only the 'fairness' characteristic of Pareto-optimality to highlight the reason why it would not be central to Islamic economics.

The reason why Islam would not necessarily accept a Pareto-optimal situation as 'fair' is that it is distributionally neutral; and that the rule is blind as to whether a person is rich or poor. To see why the Pareto-optimality rule is distributionally neutral, suppose that there are two states of the economy, x and y. The neutrality property, due to Arrow, is that if (s, t) is replaced by (v, u), then it does not materially change the nature of the social choice problem because it does not matter what the nature of s, t, v, u is. Now suppose s = equal distribution of wealth; t = nothing for person A, but equal distribution between persons B and C; v = nothing for person B and C, and all for person A; and u = equal distribution of wealth. Neutrality among these alternative states of the economy means that the extremely equal (fair) and extremely unequal (unfair) outcomes – or, in the Islamic terminology, states of the economy marked by Equilibrium (*al 'Adl* and *al Ihsan*) and those characterized by Disequilibrium (*zulm*) – are equally preferable. Thus, to the extent that it invokes the neutrality property to justify its trained incapacity to comprehend distributional issues, the relevance of the Pareto-optimality principle for Islamic economics will be correspondingly reduced. [See Naqvi (1993) for more details].

(b) That the Pareto-optimal principle cannot (literally) distinguish between the rich and the poor follows from its utilitarian character.[12] It is seen as an increasing function of the personal utility levels alone, and *all* types of non-utility information is denied admission rights as arguments of any function with which Pareto-optimality can be related. Although it may not be intuitively obvious, but this very characteristic incapacitates Pareto-optimality from differentiating the rich from the poor. The reasons are as follows. We cannot differentiate the rich from the poor on the basis of information about their respective utilities because inter-personal comparisons of utility are not allowed. We also cannot identify the poor as those with a *lower* level of utility because this kind of information cannot be generated when we insist, as we do in a neoclassical framework, on an inter-personal *non*-comparability of utility, and on the ordinal properties of such a model. Likewise, we also cannot distinguish the rich (poor) as those who have more (less) *income*, or more (less) consumer goods; for the simple reason that, because of the strict welfarism of the neoclassical model, such non-utility information is simply not available.

As the essence of Islamic reform is to establish a society based on Equilibrium, it is necessary to have analytic tools which help us in designing policies that, among others, also achieve its egalitarian objectives. In particular, such policies will be needed to effect a transfer of resources from the rich to the poor.[13] Not only that; effecting a transfer of resources from the rich to the poor amounts to carrying out the Divine commandment to restore to the poor from the rich man's wealth what properly belongs to the former as a matter of their right.[14] Obviously, in such a framework of thought, the distributionally-neutral criterion of neoclassical economics will have to be appropriately amended, if not altogether discarded.

ETHICS AND DISTRIBUTIVE JUSTICE

One of the central concerns of Islamic economics is to bring about distributive justice [see postulates (ii) and (iii) above]. Thus, all states of the economy based on Disequilibrium (*Zulm*) must be replaced by those states which satisfy the requirement of Equilibrium (*al 'Adl* and *al Ihsan*). In other words, an Islamic economy will seek to maximize 'total' welfare and not just marginal welfare – by prescribing a redistribution of income and redesigning the initial structure of private property. That being the case, what guidance does neoclassical economics have to offer to Muslim economists? Unfortunately, only a limited one. This is because of its 'trained incapacity' to address questions of distributive justice. Let us, then, examine the problem in the context of an Islamic economy.

(i) Reducing Income Inequality

The utilitarian calculus, underlying the neoclassical economic theory, is not of much help to address the problem of income distribution.[15] The utilitarian equality, which requires equalizing the *marginal* utility of everyone, is really a prescription for *inaction* because of its insistence on the non-comparability of utilities, and on ordinalism. For this reason, as noted above, it cannot 'see' the difference between the rich and the poor! In particular, once we come to the distribution of utilities, the utilitarian calculus offers only cold comfort to the poor; for, according to the utility metric, even the smallest gain in the total utility sum would be offset by the worst type of distributional inequality. The equalization of *total* utility is also an unsatisfactory concept because it does not recognize the intensity of a person's needs; and it is also insensitive to the magnitude of the potential utility gains and losses. The main problem here is that both these indices of welfare make use of utility information alone. As a result, one can easily be trapped in a situation in which *more* income is given to the less needy, simply because he is not so easily satisfied; while a poor person, who is more easily satisfied, may end up receiving *less*. But this state of affairs is unacceptable to Islamic economics.

(ii) Structural Change

With Islam's insistence on total welfare, and not just on marginal welfare, it is inevitable that a structural change will become necessary wherever the existing situation is inconsistent with the Equilibrium axiom. But, once again, neoclassical economics is not of much help because to insist on Pareto-optimality is to vote for the *status quo*, even if it be one that is based on the grossest type of distributive injustice! The first part of the Fundamental Theorem of Welfare Economics – every competitive equilibrium is Pareto-optimal – simply shows that competitive equilibrium is 'unimprovable'; and that if it co-exists with extreme poverty, then nothing can be done about it. However, the second part of the Theorem – i.e., *if initial endowments are suitably redistributed through lump-sum transfers*, the Pareto-optimal state will also approximate competitive equilibrium – does offer some room for a structural change.[16] Needless to add, for the second part of the Fundamental Theorem to indicate a change, an unjust *status quo* must entail making structural changes in the initial endowments of assets and wealth. [See Naqvi and Qadir (1985)]. But what scope is there for corrective action, given the self-interest behaviour of atomistic economic agents? Not much, unfortunately; this is because there is not enough incentive for an individual acting in his own interest to reveal such information, for the simple reason that every individual is supposed to know *only* about his *own* utility function. That being the case, the Pareto-optimal solution – that secured through a bargaining process – will not even be efficient! [Arrow, (1979)].

What, then, needs to be done? The obvious answer is to get rid of utilitarianism, and to look for an analytical structure which *prescribes* structural change. One such analysis, which rejects utilitrianism and allows for ethical considerations to enter the economic calculus, is the Rawlsian (1971) Justice-as-Fairness rule, which explicitly insists on *changing* the existing social order if it does not accord with the universally held conception of justice held by the people living in a society. Such a concept should be broadly consistent with the Islamic ethical axioms.

The Rawlsian conception is based on two basic principles of justice, which have been chosen fairly in an 'initial situation' through a procedure which guarantees impartiality – a situation in which (a) 'each person has an equal right to the most extensive liberty compatible with a like liberty for all'; and in which (b) 'inequalities are arbitrary unless it is reasonable to expect that they will work out for everyone's advantage, and provided that the position and offices to which they attach, or from which they may be gained, are open to all.'

The most attractive part of the Rawlsian analysis from an Islamic point of view is that it seeks to maximize the welfare of the worst-off individuals in the society. The Rawlsian prescription is to choose between social institutions so that *the worst-off is made the best-off*. In this scheme of things, there is no room for trading off a slight gain of the poor person for a big gain of the rich. The gain of the poor (indeed, of the poorest) comes first, whatever else may happen in a given state of the economy.

However, it should be noted that the Rawlsian criterion is *not* a principle of equality for the simple reason that it does not put limits on how much is being done at the same time for the best-off in a society in an alternative state of the economy. This aspect of the Rawlsian principle is especially not acceptable from the Islamic point of view, which seeks to limit not only the (disposable) income of the rich by transferring adequate amounts to the poor, but also the disposition of whatever (disposable) income he has. Furthermore, *Islam would seek to reduce the number of people in the worst-off income group*. The Islamic position, therefore, will be to modify the Rawlsian criterion in such a fashion that, while the relative position of the worst-off person is improved, *the number of people in this category is also reduced*.

ETHICS AND THE ROLE OF THE GOVERNMENT

Human freedom, in general, and the freedom of the economic agents, in particular, is directly derivable from the axiom of Free Will, which gives individuals the power to choose between alternative courses of action. But the course of action that is productive of the *best* result must be consistent with the principle of Equilibrium. As noted above, this principle requires taking a series of steps to rectify injustice in the basic social institutions – legal, political, and economic; it also relates to establishing a just balance between the economic activities related to the consumption, production, and distribution functions [see postulate (ii) above]. All this is done in such a manner that the needs of the least-privileged in the society get a priority over all else *and* an upper limit is put on how much the rich get in each state of the economy.

But what models incorporate such extensive constraints on economic behaviour? Is it the laissez-faire model? Obviously not, because, as is well-known, free markets run by self-interest-maximizing economic agents, who may otherwise be productively efficient, fail in many important cases to maximize social welfare. This is especially the case when achieving the social optimum requires an equitable redistribution of *legally sanctioned* private property rights. As Arrow (1979) has shown, for such a redistribution to take place through atomistic markets, each individual economic agent must reveal information about his initial endowments to other individuals – something that cannot happen in a neoclassical world because economic agents in free-markets are not supposed to know each other's utility functions. But it can be shown that, if this knowledge is absent, then any Pareto-efficient solution will not necessarily be efficient! The laissez-faire model will also fail because the Responsibility axiom will require even greater information about each other's utility functions to optimize social welfare. By the same token, the free markets fail to maximize the welfare of the least-privileged in the society.

If the *laissez-faire* model fails, would it then take a (near) complete socialization of economic activity, including that of the means of production, to meet the egalitarian goals of an Islamic economy? The socialist doctrine considers a complete passage of real resources from private hands to state control as both a necessary and a sufficient condition to maximize social welfare.[17] But such is *not* the Islamic view, which seeks to combine private initiative with government intervention in order to achieve, what Sadr (1982) calls, a 'social balance'. The state's role in the economic sphere will be fairly extensive, especially when it comes to creating a Rawls-type social order based on some principles akin to the Justice-as-Fairness prescription – in spirit, if not in letter.

Taleghani (1982) would assign a basic role to the state in restructuring the private-property rights. For instance, the state will abolish the uneconomic *and* unethical institutions like feudalism. The state's role is also essential in guaranteeing a minimum living standard to the least-privileged in the society. In general, the share of 'public goods' will rise in the Islamic society. However, it should be noted that this fact need not necessarily involve a take-over by the state of the physical production of such goods. Under certain restrictions, the private sector can be induced to produce such goods – especially because, in the Islamic society, the economic agents need not be irrevocably chained to selfishness and greed. The point to note is that taking the (Islamic) ethical requirements into consideration explicitly would necessitate a significant degree of state intervention like the one normally encountered in situations where externalities obtain without any ethical strings attached to them. It may be noted, however, that the exact mix of private-public control at any given point in time will be largely dictated by the prevalent objective conditions; it cannot be determined *a priori* on an ideological basis. (For more details of such intersystemic comparisons, see Chapter 6).

THE PROBLEM OF SOCIAL CHOICE IN AN ISLAMIC ECONOMY[18]

The foregoing discussion should make it clear that a different kind of economic behaviour will be required to accommodate the distinctive ethical rules that an Islamic economy must reflect. It will involve, for example, commitment more than egotism, trusteeship rather than absolute ownership. However, a relevant question that arises at this stage must be answered now: what does such a motivational orientation offer to resolve the problem of the impossibility of making a social choice in an Islamic economy? The question looks deceptively simple. Arrow's (1951) well-known Impossibility Theorem in effect rules out a 'non-dictatorship solution' to the problem of constructing a social preference ordering of the individuals making up the society. Within the context of its assumptions – i.e., 'unrestricted domain', Pareto-optimality, independence of irrelevant alternatives, and non-dictatorship – the Theorem's nihilism is complete with respect to the possibility of making a social choice. The basic question, then, is: how does an ethics-related Islamic economy view this 'impossibility'?

A resolution of the Impossibility Theorem lies in a demonstration of the irrelevance in an Islamic economy of one or more of the basic Arrowian postulates.[19] The problem is real since, as noted above, a 'dictatorship solution' – i.e., where any one individual's (i.e., the dictator's) preferences become the basis of social action – is *not* acceptable to Islam because of its proclamation of every individual's pre-eminence as an inviolable 'fact' of social existence. Hence, social action must not reflect the choices of just one individual. That being the case, at least two of the basic postulates of Arrow's theorem will not be satisfied in an Islamic economy – i.e., the assumption of unrestricted domain and Pareto-optimality.

According to the Islamic perception, not all of the individual preferences carry equal 'weight' as is the case in the Benthamite world of utilitarianism; indeed, some of his preferences must be assigned a zero weight.[20] And this 'weighting' is not done arbitrarily but according to a clearly laid down ethical norm – i.e., Equilibrium. Hence, not all the preferences but only those which conform to this 'norm' can be taken into consideration in deriving an appropriate social decision rule. Furthermore, since the individual's preferences are not independent of the economic processes, an 'exogenous' ethical norm like Equilibrium is required to escape the logical circularity involved in treating such preferences as determinants of the economic process. Such a procedure of 'discriminatory', but not arbitrary, weighting reduces the size of Arrow's 'unrestricted domain' – i.e., the individual preference set, over which 'aggregation' has to be performed to yield a meaningful social choice.[21] That such a procedure leads to a 'just' solution should be obvious when it is remembered that, in the Islamic perception, *social action must be geared directly to the amelioration of the least-privileged in the society*. This leads to the second point: the Islamic system would violate Arrow's assumption of Pareto-optimality. Instead, in it, the weighted individual preferences will be ordered in a lexicographic fashion. Since two of the four conditions postulated by Arrow are violated, social choice in an Islamic economy, which seeks to maximize the individual and social welfares simultaneously, is 'possible'.

SUMMARY

An *obligation* to mix ethics with economics has far-reaching consequences for economic behaviour in an Islamic economy. The Islamic ethical axioms, and the basic postulates identified at the beginning of this chapter, should clarify what we may expect. To begin with, 'rational' behaviour could never be conterminous with the self-interest maximization behaviour of economic agents; so that different individuals need not work in *complete* ignorance about each other's utility functions. Rational behaviour will then be re-defined to take into consideration the moral obligations as well. This is both a matter of belief (in Islamic metaphysics) and of actually acting generally in accordance with it. Once rational behaviour is re-defined in such a manner, a good deal of neoclassical economic theory will have to be reworked. In particular, the Pareto-optimality principle will not be the cornerstone of Islamic economics – at least not when questions of equity and a fair distribution of income and wealth have to be resolved. This is *because* the former sticks to an unjust *status quo*; in the latter, economic institutions must change when they are manifestly unjust.

One aspect of this course of action is to help the least-privileged in the society in all states of the economy. But that kind of insistence knocks out the concept of the utility function, which will not even be defined once consumer preferences are lexicographically ordered. Indeed, the metric of utility as a measure of individual welfare will also have to give way to a more comprehensive measure of individual welfare, one that comes about when individual welfare is seen in relation to the entire set of institutions which define a 'just' economic order.

These considerations also make it obvious that the models which idealize a laissez-faire type of institution, or those which are based on a complete regimentation of economic life, are both inadequate representations of the behaviour of economic agents in a typical Muslim society. That being the case, one does not visualize an Islamic economy in terms of a continuum of (perfect) and free (private) markets, but one where both the private and the public sectors work towards an interface according to the axiom of Equilibrium, which consists of the ethical and the economic factors in equal measure.

NOTES

1 This is not to say that the Christian or other religious communities do not take their religions seriously. All that we are saying is that the Muslim's beliefs are significantly different from those of the others; and, perhaps, the influence of religious beliefs is more decisive in Muslim society than in any other society. See Boisard (1987).
2 The matter has been dealt with at length in the economic literature. See, for example, Sen (1987). Here we discuss the issue from the Islamic point of view.
3 Going a step further, at a 'higher' level of spirituality, a Muslim would be acting not for a material reward but *only* for seeking God's pleasure: 'We feed you for the sake of Allah only. We wish for no reward nor thanks from you' (76:9).
4 Parts of the discussion in this section draw on Naqvi (1981a). See also Nazeer (1982), and Nasr (1987).
5 A few examples should demonstrate this point: (i) Smith (1776)

THE RULES OF ECONOMIC BEHAVIOUR IN AN ISLAMIC ECONOMY

maintained: 'It is not from the benevolence of the butcher, the brewer, or the baker, that we expect our dinner, but from their regard to their self-interest' (p. 26); (ii) Robbins (1932) laid down: 'It does not seem logically possible to associate the two studies [ethics and economics] in any form but mere juxtaposition. Economics deals with ascertainable facts; ethics with valuations and obligations' (p. 132) (iii) More recently, Stigler (1981) has passed a corroborating verdict on the matter: 'Let me predict the outcome of the systematic and comprehensive testing of behaviour in situations where self-interest and ethical values with wide verbal allegiance are in conflict. Much of the time, most of the time, in fact, the self-interest theory (as I interpret it on the Smithian lines) will win' (p. 76). But as Stigler has not reported doing any survey or opinion poll on the question, his opinion is more an example of rationalizing a *belief* in the absolute superiority of the market-based solutions – or at best a convenient simplification – rather than a piece of empirical reasoning.

6 Indeed, if this assumption is relaxed – e.g., if the consumer ranks the states of the economy by a *lexicographical* ordering of his commodity bundles – then the 'convex' world of neoclassical consumer theory will simply melt away. See, for instance, Quirk and Saposnik (1968).

7 Sen (1987) points out that 'the self-interest view of rationality involves a firm rejection of the ethical-related view of motivation'. Thus an explicit recognition of the latter view should cause considerable commotion among the protagonists of the former view.

8 In the philosophical literature, the dichotomous character of man is also seen in terms of 'well-being' and 'agency'. See Sen (1985).

9 Discontinuous behaviour is involved only if two states of economy, *a* and *b*, have identical amounts of good A, and that a consumer prefers *b* over *a*, where *b* has more of B. See Quirk and Saposnik (1968). If this be the case, a utility function will simply not exist. This proposition is formally proved in Debreu (1959).

10 A necessary and sufficient condition for a state of economy to be Pareto-optimal is that it is no longer possible to raise everyone's welfare, so that the welfare of person A cannot be increased without lowering the welfare of person B.

11 However, the Pareto-optimality principle acquires a more benign look if treated as a 'core' or 'value' because such reformulations of the principle explicitly stipulate a perfect redistribution of property rights. [Khan (1991)]. But the looks become suspect once equity is defined, *à la* Rawls, as involving a redistribution of property rights serving to help the least privileged in the society as a precondition of a just social order – which is the hallmark of Islamic economics.

12 The discussion in this and the previous sections is based on Sen (1983).

13 This would be in pursuance of the Quranic injunction, 'And in whose wealth a due share is included for the needy and those dispossessed' (70: 24–25).

14 The text refers to the Quranic verse (16:71)] wherein the words 'restore' and 'right' appear. See footnote 13 of Chapter 6.
15 In some modern treatments of the growth theory and the uncertainty theories, the cardinal utility principle has re-emerged. An interesting example is Diamond and Mirrlees (1971).
16 This clarification is due to Sen (1987).
17 For instance, this is so according to Aleshina (1976).
18 This section is based on Naqvi (1981b).
19 That Arrow's Impossibility Theorem will not remain relevant when one or more of its four basic assumptions are not satisfied is clearly brought out in Sen (1970), Chapter 9.
20 The Benthamite principle does not 'grade' happiness: 'equality of pleasure being equal, push-pin is as good as poetry'. See Russell (1964).
21 Simon (1957) argues that the task of deriving social choice from the individual choices should be done more meaningfully with respect to a subset of alternatives which are influenced by social and psychological – and, I may add, ethical – factors. This definition makes more sense than worrying, as Arrow does, about a 'complete' preference ordering of the individuals. See also Hahn and Hollis (1979).

6
A PERSPECTIVE ON INTER-SYSTEMIC COMPARISONS

In order to highlight the basic characteristics of the Islamic economy, we compare it at a theoretical level with capitalism, socialism, and the welfare state. But making such inter-systemic comparisons is not the same thing as identifying the Islamic economy with these economic systems. This is because the superficial impressions made on the basis of isolated dissimilarities between the economic systems can be quickly demolished by citing even more persuasive inter-system similarities. Hence, we need objective criteria for evaluating different economic systems *in relation to the Islamic economic system*. The axiomatic approach presented in this book provides such a set of objective criteria. With its help, it should be possible to establish analytically the distinctive character of an ethically-oriented Islamic economic system, steering clear of its misplaced and confusing associations with other economic systems.

Four points should be noted about this exercise. First, the argument to distinguish the Islamic economy from capitalism, socialism or the welfare state by reference to Islam's ethical values is intended to establish its superiority over its rivals only from the point of view of a representative Muslim – i.e. that, other things being equal, he would tend to *prefer* an economic system that is in accord with his ethical beliefs. It is not necessarily a detailed demonstration of the superiority of the former over the latter in some absolute sense. Second, whenever such an absolute *superiority* is asserted, it is just another illustration of the main theme of this book – that a theoretical system combining economic considerations and moral values will presumably be superior to one that prides on its exclusive positivism. Third, making such a comparison does not imply a wholesale condemnation of socialism or capitalism. Both the systems have worked with success; and there is a lot that a real-life Islamic economic system will have to learn from these systems – in particular from their vectorial vision of economic (and social) progress; from socialism, the emphasis on social and distributive justice; from capitalism, the accent on accumulation and growth within the framework of individual freedom. And, of course, the welfare-state principle will need to be examined closely for its success in combining growth with equity and individual freedom with social responsibility. But it is asserted that when these elements of success are infused with an ethical perspective, Islam may *then* have to offer something distinctive, even superior, not only to Muslims but also to the rest of mankind. Fourth, in the absence of a real-life Islamic economic system with a fairly long history, the inter-systemic comparisons presented below have been made with caution. Thus, we do not compare the ideals of the Islamic system with the practices of capitalism, socialism or the welfare state.

ISLAM AND SOCIALISM

Is the Islamic economy close to a socialist (communist) economic system? On the basis of some apparent systemic similarities, one may answer this question in the affirmative.[1] Thus, socialism may appear attractive because it explicitly addresses the problems of an equitable distribution of income and wealth, deals directly with the phenomena of poverty and hunger, and shows a deep sense of responsibility to the least privileged in the society. To achieve these objectives, the socialist remedy has been to abolish the institution of private property in all forms, including that of the means of production.[2] At a more general level, some of the Marxian insights have become part and parcel of the accepted wisdom on how societies develop over time – e.g., that the quality of tensions among economic interests has an important influence on the course and intensity of political struggles; that economic factors exercise a deep, though not necessarily a decisive, influence on historical evolution; that (capitalist) market economies are inevitably prone to recurrent economic crises. Also, the Marxian theory of surplus value – though not the Marxian theory of value, which is false – has served to focus attention on the fact of social exploitation in capitalist societies by linking the process of production and exchange with the rate of the capitalist's profit. Another attractive feature of the Marxian philosophy is its emphasis on the essential relativity of economic laws to the nature of a society; and its emphasis that such laws lose relevance once the underlying social framework has dramatically changed.

Yet, to equate socialism with the Islamic economy will be a *non sequitur*. This is because, in the Marxian vision, economic achievements are in no way related *explicitly* to any known ethical philosophy even though moral considerations are allowed to influence consciousness.[3] Indeed, the socialism calling itself 'scientific' rests its claim for recognition on the laws of dialectical materialism, not on ethical imperatives, which are seen as contingent to the prevailing economic conditions. On the other hand, in the Islamic perspective, the social fabric is made not *only* by economic forces (the Marxian relations of production); but, even more basically, it is made of a strong ethical fibre. Thus, deriving inspiration from two radically different ethical conceptions, the social institutions and structures of the Islamic society will naturally be different from those of a socialist society – at an ideological plane as also in the real world. For example, while individuals in both the systems are called upon by the governments to make sacrifices for the good of the society, the character of the individual's response to such calls in each system would be very different. Under socialism, the state curtails individual freedom for the sake of the society; but it does so arbitrarily and excessively because individual freedom, according to this system, is not an absolute value. It is, at best, an instrumental value. Contrarily, in the Islamic perspective, the freedom of an individual to make a choice between alternative options is both an absolute value and an instrumental value – it is absolute, insofar as it is based on the Free Will axiom; it is also relative, to the extent that the 'best' form of individual freedom is one that is not inconsistent with the welfare of the poor in the society – which is based on the Responsibility axiom. For this reason, when an Islamic state asks its citizens to make sacrifices, they would give due weight to moral imperatives and do so voluntarily.

Secondly, the total negation of the institution of private property under socialism is against Islam's middle-of-the-road stand on the issue.[4] Unlike the socialist philosophy, Islam gives the individual a right to own property in proportion to his own and his offspring's needs and their capacity to use it productively – 'relatively absolute' because it puts restrictions on disposing of the same, so that the property-owner does not squander his wealth out of insensitivity to the needs of the poor in the society.[5] Another restriction on ownership is that while the individual's right to own private property is respected in Islam through his lifetime, this right terminates on his death, after which the right of disposition is regulated by the Islamic laws of inheritance.[6] On the other hand, having no elaborate perception of an individual's freedom, socialism is uninhibited in totally denying this basic right to the individual.

Thirdly, the *weltanschauung* that inspires socialism is radically different from that which moves Islam to action. The impulse to economic progress, according to socialism, comes from a dialectical-historical view of the social processes to which class struggle is central: 'the history of humankind is the history of class struggle' [Marx (1848)]. True, the role of coercive factors and violence is downgraded in the Marxian dialectical vision, yet it is associated with it as a logical necessity of the class struggle that necessarily precedes social change; while sometimes it is employed to further the cause of social revolution. By contrast, Islam emphasizes a social balance, according to which economic progress need not always be born of social conflict and class war. That does not mean that economic progress will not require a resolution of conflict situations arising from the multiplicity of interest groups. Indeed, the Quran does recognize the existence of an oppressed class (*Mustadafin*) and an oppressor class (*Mustakbarin*); and in case there is a conflict between them, the Islamic injunction is to side with the oppressed. This is the Responsibility axiom at work, acting as a stabilizing force.

Fourthly, according to the Marxian dialectics, the social relations of production ultimately *determine* the patterns of thought and the level of consciousness in a society. Thus, Marx remarked in a famous passage: 'it is not the consciousness of men that determines their existence, but, on the contrary, their social existence determines their consciousness'.[7] In other words, it is not the quality of the consciousness of men that determines a particular shape of social reality; but it is the forces of production that determine social reality. And this determination comes about when the forces of production get stabilized and reproduce themselves over time, thus transforming into (semi-) fixed social structures that which can be changed only by a revolution. [Mandell (1990)]. The point to note is that the Marxian vision of social change is strictly positivistic and *dominated* by economic forces. Indeed, in this deterministic vision, an individual's free will plays at best a second fiddle. [Aron (1968); Mandell (1990)]. In sharp contrast, the Islamic viewpoint is that the level of consciousness about the social reality is determined in a decisive way by the choice made by individuals, exercising their free will. Also, the force of ideas – especially the ideas formed under the umbrella of the Prophetic revelation – is decisive in social formations. The relations of production develop both due to endogenous forces and also in response to the changing needs of the society; there is nothing deterministic about it.[8] At best such a development can be construed as a historical tendency – not a historical necessity, à la Marx, which can be rectified by timely action.

Fifthly, socialism is at best ambivalent about the role of the individual versus that of the state. Although, on the one hand, the Marxian vision clearly prohibits setting the state against the individual and envisages the withering away of the state as a logical necessity of its dialectics, yet the subjugation of the individual's free will in this historical scheme strengthens in a deterministic fashion the controlling hand of the state. Thus, in effect, socialism is consistent with both a monolithic state and anarchy.[9] Islam, on the other hand, assigns appropriate roles in the economic sphere to both the individual and the state in order to encourage private initiative and reward individual effort, without compromising social welfare.[10] The general Islamic position is to guarantee individual freedom, but with the restriction that its exercise does not injure the freedom of others, and that it does not take the individual beyond the pale of ethical norms of behaviour generally accepted by the society.

ISLAM AND CAPITALISM

If Islam is not socialism, does it then resemble capitalism in any significant way? One obvious point of agreement between the Islamic economy and capitalism is that both reject socialism. Then, there are some apparent similarities between the two systems with respect to their strongly supportive attitudes towards individual freedom and private property rights, and some agreement with regard to the growth-promoting role of private initiative. Also, Islam shares capitalism's emphasis on accumulation, in the form of commodities that can be exchanged, (rather than its use-value), as part and parcel of the overall dynamics of economic advance. Both condemn feudalism as anti-progress and favour, instead, a fluid social structure.

But, the differences between the two systems are equally, indeed more, fundamental. They arise from a common source – namely, their respective ethical perceptions.[11] While the leading proponents of capitalism continue to insist on the moral invulnerability of (exclusive) self-interest behaviour both in theory and practice,[12] the Islamic economy would not accept the unquestioned sovereignty of self-interest behaviour in the economic universe – even though the importance of such behaviour as a motivational force behind private initiative is duly recognized.[13] Thus, in contrast to capitalism's possessiveness with respect to the ownership of one's wealth, Islam emphasizes a more giving attitude. It may be noted that an acceptance of this view is not so much a restriction on the absoluteness of the individual's right to private property once certain legal requirements have been satisfied; it is rather indicative of the Islamic ethical position on the matter, according to which all wealth belongs to God, Who desires that it be owned equitably by all mankind.

It is well to remember that capitalism may denote *either* (i) the capitalist mode of production *or* (ii) the capitalist socio-economic framework [Rodinson (1978)]. These two aspects are related but also separable. Now, if the capitalist mode of production is one which vertically integrates the production processes from the primary stage to the final product stage, then this will be the essential process of industrialization in an Islamic economy also. Insofar as the capitalist socio-economic framework features (private) consumers and (private) producers as linked together through the market, this is also to be a feature of an Islamic economy. This is because Islam lays great store by individual initiative, even if the government will intervene to maximize social welfare.

But, there is another aspect of capitalism as a socioeconomic framework that needs to be noted. Capitalism is not just 'an economic system ... but as a larger cultural setting in which the pursuit of wealth served the same unconscious purposes as did the military glory ... in earlier aspects' [Heilbroner (1987)]. And something more: the capitalist system also has an ethical system of its own. According to Viner (1978), the Protestant ethics has been the driving force of capitalism: '... a dedicated and unlimited pursuit of wealth through unremitting industry, rigid limitation of expenditures on personal consumption or charity, concentration of time and attention on the pursuit of one's business affairs, avoidance of distraction through intimate friendship with others, systematic and pitiless exploitation of labour and strict observance of honesty in one's relations with others within the limits set by "formal legality" ' (p. 151).[14] Thus, the capitalists' wealth accumulated rapidly, while exploitative wages and wretched labour conditions prevailed in the heyday of capitalism – a process that clearly illustrates the Marxian prescription according to which profits and the competitive rate of profit is determined by surplus value, which in turn measures the size of social exploitation involved in the capitalist system.

Aside from the problems of implementation, which are discussed later in this book, in principle Islam would seek to minimize the exploitation of labour by seeking a fair functional distribution of income. It would also not look favourably on the accumulation of wealth by a few capitalists as an absolute virtue, without regard to its social consequences. To see this inter-systemic difference more clearly, the following points may be noted. First, from the Islamic point of view, the over-emphasis of capitalism on material values upsets the delicate balance between ethical and economic behaviours. Indeed, under capitalism, the individual's self-interest maximizing behaviour supersedes any meaningful value system, especially that based on religion. By contrast, in Islam, the urge to accumulate wealth has been reduced on the scale of human values and subordinated to an overarching vision which gives due weight to non-monetary and moral values as well: 'Wealth and children are an ornament of life of the world. But the good deeds which endure are better in thy Lord's sight for reward, and better in respect of hope' (18:47).

Secondly, contrary to capitalism's (moral) sanction to accumulate wealth without any clear-cut limitations, Islam clearly recognizes that a part of an individual's wealth properly belongs to the poor, and that they (the poor) are deprived of this part by the social organization of production. In such cases, Islam recommends remedial action so that the poor get their due share.[15] It may be noted that Islam recognizes some differentials in the earning capacities of different individuals insofar as these flow from differences in the inputs of work effort and intellectual capacities; but it puts restrictions on the disposition of wealth, and also on the 'surplus' of income that flows from the production of socially non-profitable goods.

Thirdly, capitalism insists on the individual's economic freedom; and an important element of this freedom is the individual's right to private property, and especially his right 'to *withhold* it from the use of society if they so wish.' [Heilbroner (1987)]. While these capitalistic rights may have been necessary for individual liberty and social progress, it will be wrong to assert on this basis that capitalism is *sufficient* for the achievement of these goals. Thus, alternative economic systems can also accomplish the same. Thus, in the Islamic society, individual freedom flows from the concept of Free Will – which is founded on the belief that all property belongs to God, and that man holds it only in trust for Him.[16] Furthermore, Islam does not extend unqualified support to the institution of private property as a matter of absolute (procedural) right of the individual owner because of its consequence-sensitive social and economic philosophy – especially, with respect to the effects of the exercise of private property rights on the least-privileged in the society, whose claim on the society's wealth comes first in all states of the economy.

Fourthly, while capitalism also forces a sense of social responsibility on individuals through policies like progressive income taxes and death duties, the concept of social responsibility does not feature as centrally there as it does in an Islamic economy. While the poor do not have a *right* on the wealth of the rich under capitalism, Islam has an elaborate theory of individual's social obligations, according to which the individual must return from his wealth the dues of the society; the rich cannot squander their wealth because those who do so are 'brothers of the devil' – all this is unique to Islam and sets it apart from capitalism (as also from socialism).

ISLAM AND THE WELFARE-STATE DOCTRINE

In view of their common, distinctly egalitarian character, the Islamic economy and the welfare-state doctrine have often been equated together.[17] In a historical perspective, the welfare-state doctrine, which seeks to strike a middle course between capitalism and socialism, is seen as a culmination of the struggle for political citizenship rights. [T.H. Marshall (1963)]. While insisting on individual freedom, it seeks to inculcate a sense of responsibility in the society by ensuring that individuals and families are enabled to meet certain basic contingencies – sickness, old age, unemployment – irrespective of the market value of their property. (Briggs (1961)]. Through a heavy taxation of the rich, an elaborate welfare system – also referred to as 'fiscal welfare' – provides health, education and other basic facilities to the have-nots. Thus, while the inequalities of income are permitted at the (gross) earnings level, income equalization occurs in terms of the disposable (after-tax) income. A conscious attempt is also made not to let income differentials grow too large.

Fundamentally, the welfare-state doctrine derives its character from the socialistic principle: 'From everyone according to his ability and to everyone according to his needs.' This principle effects a separation between the capacity of a *few* individuals to earn and the entitlement of *every* individual in the society to a minimum standard of living.[18] Thus, state intervention becomes necessary to regulate production as well as consumption in a capitalist market economy. [Gough (1989)].[19] In sharp contrast, the system of free markets, as stipulated under capitalism, does not contain built-in guarantees to satisfy either of these two rules.

The ethical basis of the Islamic economy, which seeks to tread the 'middle' path denoted by Equilibrium,[20] points in the same direction – with even greater force, because it seeks to combine state coercion with the force of voluntaristic urges of man. For instance, in spending one's wealth, Islam enjoins that the individuals be 'neither prodigal nor miserly in their spending but follow a middle path' (25:67). The Islamic approach is to permit some inequalities of income but to put restriction on expenditure, the difference between income and expenditure going to the poor. Once again, the aim is 'that it [wealth] does not concentrate in the hands of those who are rich among you' (59:7). Within the Islamic framework, egotistic behaviour is combined with commitment, the principle of absolute ownership is replaced by that of trusteeship, and the needs of the least privileged become the *first* charge on the nation's resources. Furthermore, the Quranic verse, 'And in their wealth the beggar and the deprived had due share' (51:19), lays down the 'separability' of consumption from the individual's capacity to earn. To bridge this gap, a conscious redistributive policy, equalizing income and wealth marginally as well as intra-marginally, is clearly required.[21]

Such differences as there are between the Islamic economy and the welfare-state doctrine have a fundamental bearing not only on what individuals consider as 'rational' behaviour, but on the entire spectrum of economic activities – i.e., consumption, production, and distribution. Indeed, the very 'character' of the social welfare function undergoes a profound change. Thus, if there is a choice, an Islamic state will not reduce social expenditure while increasing other types of expenditure. By the same token, the equilibrium positions will be characterized by a distinctive 'consumption' basket, excluding those commodities whose consumption has been banned in Islam, while including more of those goods which are consumed by the poor – i.e., the wage goods. To provide for an increase in the demand for wage goods, the production structure will also have to be oriented differently. These differences will remain even if (as is not unlikely) the distribution of income and wealth is similar under these two egalitarian economic systems, and even though both emphasize human freedom and responsibility.

SUMMARY

The inter-systemic comparisons presented in this chapter highlight the originality of the Islamic viewpoint on economics, notwithstanding the many points of similarity between different economic systems. The Islamic economy is defined within the parameters of its own ethical system, which fact, incidentally, demonstrates its originality and relativity. Unlike any other system, the ethical impulses are fully integrated with economic motives in the Islamic economy. Thus, the many restrictions put on consumption and production, and the many directives to redistribute wealth, are enforced mostly on a *voluntary* basis precisely because the legitimate economic pursuits are not separable from spiritual achievements. Once this central feature of Islamic economics is understood, there is no possibility of confusing it with capitalism, socialism, or the welfare state. While the truth of Islamic economics is necessarily relative, it also has a universal character. One can detect strong affinities between the Islamic egalitarian principles and the welfare-state doctrine, as well as the equally strong points of difference between the two.

However, it should be noted that a mere demonstration that the Islamic economic system will be preferred by the Muslims to socialism and capitalism *does not necessarily mean that in real-world situations such a preference will in fact be exercised*. For that to happen, a real-world Islamic economic system, when it is established, will have to face the challenge of the existing economic systems – capitalism and socialism. To make sure that Muslims do in fact exercise this preference, the Islamic system will have to do better than the other systems in ensuring economic growth with distributive justice, explicitly recognizing the needs of the least-privileged in the society. This will *not* come about just by pointing out the Divine *nature* of the Islamic economic system but by its success in achieving the Divine *purpose* in the modern world.

But to do this, the aims and objectives of the Islamic economy will need to be clearly laid out, and the policy instruments designed to achieve them will have to be carefully chosen – allowing a lot of room for flexibility and innovation in the choice of both the ends and the means. It is to this task that we now turn in the following chapters.

NOTES

1 See, for instance, al-Sibai's (?) influential work for a strongly positive answer.
2 But, of late, the institution of private property is being revived in the communist countries.
3 In the Marxian vision, every society has its own *infra-structure* which consists of the forces and the relation of production; it also possesses its *superstructure* 'wherein figure the legal and political institutions as well as ways of thinking, and philosophies' [Aron (1968)].
4 Thus Boisard (1987) states: 'If, for example, [in Islam] private prop-

erty and individual initiative are recognized as opposed to collective communism, they are strictly limited, which is contrary to Western liberalism' (p. 110).
5 The Quran categorically states: 'Squander not your wealth among yourselves in vanity' (4:29).
6 For a detailed discussion of these issues, see Taleghani (1982).
7 Marx (1859): Preface. He presented the same thesis earlier in response to Hegel's emphasis on the intellectual, spiritual, conceptual or religious as determinants of history: 'In direct contrast to German philosophy which descends from heaven to earth, here we ascend from earth to heaven ... life is not determined by consciousness, but consciousness by life' [Marx and Engels (1845-6)].
8 As a proof of the *non-dialectic* character of the Islamic economic philosophy, Sadr (1982) notes that the Islamic position on the equality of men in the eyes of God, on the pattern of property rights, and on a score of similar matters about which an elaborate structure of Islamic law exists could not have been *determined* by the primitive modes of production in the Arabian society existing at the time of the advent of Islam.
9 Lindblom (1977) notes that, though committed to the goal of economic equality, communist countries 'never aspired to political equality and have in fact disclaimed it in order to justify concentrating political authority in a ruling "elite" ' (5, p. 266).
10 Taleghani (1982) remarks: 'there is [in Islam] private ownership based on the innate and natural freedom of individuals, and collective ownership based on public resources and interests' (p. 25).
11 For a somewhat different, and at times the opposite, view, see Rodinson (1978), especially Chapter 5.
12 Evaluating the role of ethics in economics, Stigler (1981) concludes: '... We live in a world of reasonably well-informed people acting intelligently in pursuit of their self-interests' (p. 190).
13 For instance, Taleghani (1982) points out that 'Islamic economics is based neither on the unlimited freedom of private ownership that leads to unbridled capitalism nor on public ownership that results in total denial of individual ownership and freedom ...' (p. 25).
14 See also Aron (1970) for an evaluation of the Weberian thesis.
15 According to some Muslim scholars, the Quranic verse – 'God has favoured some of you with more provision than others. Yet those of you who have more do not *return* of their means to those whom their right hand possesses [are inferior to them] *so that they may not become their equals*. Will they deny then God's beneficence?' (16:77) (Italics added) – is a clear pointer to Islam's original philosophy whereby, while the rich may be the initial recipients of income, a part of it belongs to the poor *as a matter of moral right*. Hence, those who earn more must *return* it to the poor. And those who do not do so for fear that their inferiors will become their equals are in fact denying God's beneficence. For a similar interpretation of this verse, see Jauhri (1984).
16 The concept of trusteeship in the Islamic ethical context simply

means that the private ownership of wealth should be freed from excessive greed and selfishness; and that it be made consistent with social welfare. Above all, these restrictions on private ownership are supposed to be voluntarily imposed by the individuals on themselves in obedience to God's Will.

17 The term welfare state, was first used in English language in 1941. The concept has, however, been around longer in several strands of European thought. In Britain, Syndicalism tried to achieve a balance between the power of the State and individual freedom. In Germany, the concept *wohlfahrstat* was introduced in 1920 and denoted the modern social insurance system. It rejected both the unqualified support of capitalism to the institution of private property and the excessive collectivistic tendencies of socialism. However, it could not really get off to a start as a practical action programme. See Russell (1977). In the Scandinavian countries, there has been a long tradition of combining individual freedom with social responsibility, by insisting on a socialistic economic programme along with political democracy. The results have been satisfactory in terms of achieving a moderate economic growth and an egalitarian income distribution.

18 Thus welfare state is also defined as 'the use of state power to modify the reproduction of labour power and to maintain the non-working propulations in capitalist societies' [Gough (1979)].

19 State intervention may take the form of an appropriate tax-cum-subsidy policy to achieve the social optimum in production. However, it may also become necessary to create government-sponsored institutions to effect an appropriate redistribution of income and wealth and to provide the sick, the old, and the needy with a minimum level of consumption.

20 In fact, the Muslim nation has been characterized in the Quran as 'the people of the "middle" [way]'. 'We have appointed you a middle nation . . .' (2:143). Some translators of the Quran substitute 'best' for 'middle', denoting the middle course as the best course, since it is the path to attain Equilibrium. However, let it be noted that this path is not necessarily the middle path between capitalism and socialism.

21 Shafi (1968) states the same principle: 'According to the Islamic point of view, not only those who have directly participated in the production of wealth but those to whom Allah has made it obligatory upon others to help, are the legitimate sharers in wealth' (p. 8). Naqvi (1978) makes the same point.

Part III

THE OBJECTIVES AND POLICIES IN AN ISLAMIC ECONOMY

7
SETTING THE POLICY OBJECTIVES

The next logical step taken in this and the subsequent chapters is to derive from the basic ethical postulates – and from a few additional hypotheses set out in Chapters 3 and 4 – the basic objectives of the Islamic economy. It will be recalled from Chapter 2 that the concept of Muslim society was introduced to provide Islamic economics with an empirical base, where its hypotheses could be verified some day.[1] We do not need to verify the objectives of an Islamic economy in order to spell them out; all that we need to do is to establish that they are consistent with the basic ethical postulates. Thus, the argument can be conducted strictly on a logical plane; but such an exercise becomes meaningful only in a real-world context. Hence, in this and the following chapters, all statements about the *Islamic* economy also hold for *Muslim* society.

The analysis presented in the preceding chapters raises definite expectations. For instance, as a logical corollary of the Equilibrium axiom, one would expect that an Islamic economy will look for an explicit mechanism to ensure a reasonably fast rate of growth of per capita income with distributive justice in order to offer meaningful solutions to the problems of extreme poverty and inequality in the distribution of income and wealth; and that social organization of production, consumption, and distribution decisions will be reorientated to achieve these objectives. The Islamic economy will accord priority to justice in choosing from among the alternative states of a growing economy; and any inequities that are tolerated will be for the sake of achieving better equity levels in the long run (through higher growth). In that connection, one would also expect that human capital formation will be emphasized as much as physical capital formation, and employment opportunities will be provided to meet the demand for these (in the labour market).

THE BASIC OBJECTIVES

It is asserted in this chapter that at least five policy objectives can be derived from the basic Islamic ethical postulates – namely, individual freedom, distributive justice, economic growth, universal education, and maximum employment generation. Now we turn to a detailed discussion of these points.

Individual Freedom

As discussed in Chapter 2, the concept of individual freedom in Islam is fundamental. It derives from the 'fact' that man has been invested with a 'free will', whence follows his vicegeral virtuality and his innate freedom to choose between the different courses of action open to him. But as he exercises his freedom, the 'most' rational course of action open to an individual will be to avoid socially explosive situations where the exercise of individual rights co-exists with extreme poverty and human misery. Once this point of view is explicitly understood, the economic agent will be inclined to care for social welfare as well while looking after his personal welfare – if only because he wants to avoid the envy of the have-nots. It is not a question of one or the other but a happy combination of the two which will guarantee maximum happiness for the individual and the society.

There are several points about the Islamic concept of human freedom which should be noted carefully.

Firstly, as noted in Chapter 3, the Islamic viewpoint is different from the (Kantian) concept of the 'absolute autonomy' of man.[2] Accepting that absolute autonomy is enjoyed only by God, man's autonomy can only be *relative*. But it should be carefully noted that, *as between individuals*, the Islamic 'relatively absolute' autonomy weighs at least as much as the Kantian absolute autonomy.

Secondly, the quantity and the quality of human freedom are determined by the interaction between Free Will and Responsibility, which also define the limits on the quality of human choice meant to produce the 'best' social outcome. The authoritarianism implicit in this view should be moderate because man finds his true freedom, interpreted broadly, only by observing the laws and regulations framed for the smooth working of the social organization.[3] In this respect, the Islamic concept of individual freedom contrasts with that trend in Western 'liberal' thought which argues for a 'minimal' state and is against all attempts by the government to 'pattern' distributional outcomes resulting from the exercise of individual rights.[4] Instead, the Islamic view is closer to the liberal tradition that considers a welfare-oriented society to be a logical extension of the (political) citizenship rights.[5]

Thirdly, the limits on human freedom to choose between alternative options pertain to keeping a 'balance' between the claims of different individuals and classes on the nation's total produce. Such a balance, dictated by the Equilibrium postulate, can be achieved by the observance of the following two principles:

(a) An individual is entitled to an appropriate reward for his work and acts of investment in the form of wages and profits; but the total income so earned, plus what he gets from inheritance, must be spent with moderation.[6]

(b) The needs of the poor and the needy have a prior *right* on the wealth of the (rich) individuals. The force of this principle has been strengthened by equating to the denial of Faith a wilful failure of the rich to give to the poor their right.[7]

Distributive Justice

An uncompromising insistence on distributive justice *in all states of the economy* is one of the most distinctive elements of the Islamic teachings on economics.[8] If given a choice, a state of the economy characterised by more distributive justice – defined as a superior distribution of income and wealth, in accordance with the universally accepted norms of fairness – will be preferred to the one with less distributive justice. This principle clearly illustrates the connection between ethics and economics. Thus, the (morally) right social states are those which accord priority to equity (*qist*). Such states would be characterized by a greater degree of income (and wealth) equality than those in the other social systems. However, this rule has to be interpreted in a dynamic context to make sure that an equalization of income (and wealth) today does not lower welfare tomorrow – in which case the present generation may be doing injustice to the posterity. (See the next section). Thus, as a rule, unequal distribution of income and wealth may be acceptable if (and only if) a more equal distribution of income today will lower future welfare.

Secondly, the Islamic insistence on distributive justice (and, more broadly, social justice) inevitably involves the concept of the *equality of opportunity* to ensure that the processes through which different individuals come to occupy specific stations in life are equally available to all. However, it does *not* insist on the *equality of result* in an absolute sense. In other words, Islam would permit significant though not very large differences in the rewards given to the position occupied by each person according to the productive activity he engages in.[9] However, note that the differences in earnings need not always imply corresponding differences – certainly not large differences – in the *consumption* capability of different individuals.[10]

Thirdly, the requirement of distributive justice entails, as a rule, that man must receive what is due him by virtue of his productive effort.[11] But *since the equality of all men before God implies the equality of all men in relation to each other*, those who cannot work because of sickness, old age, etc., must receive adequate income to cover their basic needs, irrespective of the level of their productive effort (which in the extreme cases of social and personal distress may be zero). Also, steps must be taken to alleviate absolute poverty and minimize gross inequalities in income and wealth in pursuance of the explicit Quranic injunctions.[12]

Fourthly, to make sure that the distributive justice ensured in terms of income becomes meaningful, it is essential that the production structure is also suitably modified so that the supply of wage goods rises significantly in the total produce. Also, in societies where agriculture is dominant, the system of land tenure and the capital and labour markets will have to be regulated to produce equitable outcomes. It may be instructive to reiterate here that the Islamic concept of distributive justice rests on the Islamic concept of man's trusteeship;[13] and that the relatively absolute right of the individual to own private property that results from this concept relates both to the disposition of wealth and to the quantum of ownership itself.[14] Given the fact that the poor have a right in the rich man's wealth, the latter can not hoard wealth.[15] As to the ownership of private property, especially of land ownership, it has been restricted in various ways. For instance, individuals cannot own uncultivated lands, forests, grazing grounds, mines, etc. All these must be owned by the public authority for public welfare.

Finally, the purpose of distributive justice is to make a net contribution to man's well-being. To this end, the attainment of human happiness is made conditional on an individual's performing good *acts*. It may be interesting to note that this view of human happiness is exactly the reverse of the Benthamite philosophy of Maximum Happiness, according to which an act is good if it maximizes happiness, which is pursued by individuals on their own.[16] In this view, happiness is whatever makes man happy, irrespective of how it comes about – thus 'a push-pin is as good as poetry.' It is so regardless of how the fruits of such (productive) acts are distributed among various classes. Translated into an operative principle, such 'relativism' can only enhance social tensions. Bentham was aware of this problem and sought to resolve it by proposing to regulate a selfish pursuit of happiness in order to reconcile it with public interest. However, this prescription sends us back to square one; we are now asked to define (or redefine) what it is that constitutes a *legitimate* pursuit of happiness. One possible way of resolving the problem is to catalogue the permissible objects of happiness; but this would be a non-terminating process. A simpler approach is to specify the acts by reference to which human happiness can be measured. An Islamic prescription for human happiness would be closer to this simpler approach.

Universal Education

The acquisition of knowledge is the most important means to actualize man's viceregal virtuality. The importance that Islam attaches to education can be seen from the fact that after the word 'Allah', the word 'knowledge' (*ilm*) is the second-most repeated word in the Quran. It is only by being a knowledgeable person (*'alim*) that man can claim superiority to the rest of God's creation. This is because knowledge is at once a means to do worldly good and to achieve spiritual salvation. Hence, Islam clearly *differentiates* between the ignorant and the knowledgeable.[17]

The most distinguishing characteristic of the Islamic society must be the high level of literacy of its members, and the (relative) high position given to its educated class. Thus, one of the basic objectives of such a society is to arrange for universal literacy and to make sure that every talented child gets the attention that he deserves to realize his intellectual potential. There is another aspect of education that must be kept in view; it is that education, especially primary education, has an (income) equalizing effect and tends to reduce poverty. However, if the initial differences in income (and wealth) are wide enough, and if the state does not subsidize education, then the 'market' will provide more education only to those who pay more. Thus, to actualize the equalizing potential, it is essential that education is subsidized – even made free for those who cannot afford it.[18] Such a policy is reinforced by the human-capital view of investment – that greater education embodied in human beings makes them more productive and thus they earn more.

Economic Growth

Economic growth would occupy a very high position in the hierarchy of objectives in an Islamic economy, because all the other objectives can be realized more fully in a strongly growing economy than in a slow-growing economy. In general, distributive justice can be achieved with less social tensions when an economy is growing fast, because then conflict situations are more easily resolved than when it is not. By creating greater employment opportunities and raising real wages (of the unskilled labour) economic growth raises real income. It is also a *necessary* condition for improving the distribution of income and wealth and reducing poverty. An economy wherein everybody gains in absolute terms – with the poor even getting a higher relative share – is clearly superior to the one in which one can gain only at the expense of the other. But growth is not a sufficient condition. Thus, income redistribution and anti-poverty programmes must be implemented to make the society more egalitarian.

It may be interesting to note that economic growth imposes a sacrifice on present generations because the posterity cannot always reciprocate the kindness of its forefathers. But this is not a violation of the principle of distributive justice, because the posterity cannot do any injustice to its parents – except in cases wherein they both interact at the same point in time. Justice can be done only within the bounds of natural limitations; it cannot transcend them. However, for the same reason, the sacrifices imposed on present generation for the sake of the posterity cannot be made arbitrarily large. Hence, economic growth should aim at a balance between the competing claims of the present and future consumptions. In other words, what the policy-maker can possibly do is to maximize an integral of the utility of the flows of consumption, or some other appropriate reference variable, over a specified period of time subject to the constraint of providing enough resources for capital formation. However, in the Islamic society, the argument (i.e., the element) of the functional will be extended to include not only material welfare but spiritual bliss as well. The inclusion in the functional of a term representing spiritual satisfaction should cause no (mathematical) problems because of its intangible character. For what is optimized, even according to neoclassical growth economics, is not the flow of consumption but the associated *utility*, which is itself an intangible quantity.[19] And the magnitude of the flow of utility will be different precisely because, in view of the binding 'allowability' constraint, the contents of the consumption basket will change substantially in an Islamic economy. Furthermore, the capital-formation constraint noted above will explicitly include human capital as well as material capital.

All these considerations may add up to a growth path which is qualitatively different from the growth paths of other economic systems – in terms of its consumption, production and distribution 'contents'. What makes it distinctive is that *at all times* the needs of 'the needy and the deprived' will have to have a first claim on the nation's produce. This restriction will imply, among other things, that the flow of wage goods consumed by the poor must grow over time, and also that the share of public goods is not allowed to diminish over time. There is a deeper philosophical reason why such a growth strategy is to be preferred. It is because the sacrifice imposed by growth, and its rewards, will then be *voluntarily* (and equitably) borne by different sections of the society.

Another aspect of the growth process is that it should be

sustainable – it should not lead to excessive depletion of renewable (and non-renewable) natural resources. In particular, the excessive pollution that certain forms of growth have caused – and Western nations have been the worst polluters – has posed a serious threat to man's survival on earth, including the dangerous thinning out of the ozone layer.[20] The point is that while to some extent such after-effects of economic growth are inevitable, a more ethically-oriented approach can save the world from a veritable environmental disaster. The basic defect of the amoral approach to economic issues arises from the 'purely antagonistic attitude towards nature' [Nasr (1976)]. The Islamic approach, on the other hand, flows from its precepts about Unity and Equilibrium – the former forging an integral view of man and nature, while the latter insisting on keeping a sense of proportion and balance in the use of science and technology – a realization that has now dawned on the world community.

Maximizing Employment Generation

Economic growth facilitates the attainment of distributive justice partly by creating more (new) employment opportunities than is possible in a static economy. The important point is that, *because of Islam's uncompromising insistence on ethical values*, a high unemployment rate cannot be a matter of (relative) unconcern in an Islamic economy, as it is in a 'capitalist' economy. Thus, when there is a trade-off between efficiency and employment, an Islamic economy would seek a balance between these objectives. To see the importance of this somewhat self-evident point, it may be noted that unemployment is *not* a very pressing issue according to 'liberal' thought, which advocates an exclusive reliance on the market outcome irrespective of the level of unemployment. Thus, if there is large unemployment, this need not indicate a failure of the (capitalist) economic system based on free markets; it is rather of a transitional variety, so that the problem is *assumed* to go away as economic growth picks up.[21]

But making employment a basic objective does not mean that it must be increased inefficiently; instead, additional employment should be generated in a *technically efficient fashion*.[22] But efficient employment generation requires that, whenever possible, the incremental capital-output ratio should be kept lower rather than higher, because the labour required per unit of capital is greater in the former case than in the latter case. This can partly be ensured through technological progress focused on evolving a suitable technology in line with resource endowment.[23]

The argument that in the Islamic society higher employment should be generated mainly by lowering the capital/labour ratio is supported by the requirement of paying a 'just' wage to the workers. While it cannot be defined in abstract terms, the need to maintain Equilibrium should specify (in broad qualitative terms) both the upper and the lower bounds of the level of a just wage: the market wage will not be 'exploitative' on *either* side of the market.

SUMMARY

Human freedom, distributive justice, universal education, economic growth, and maximum employment generation are the key policy objectives of an Islamic economy. These objectives follow directly from the basic Islamic ethical axioms and the additional hypotheses identified in Chapter 5. While human freedom is sacrosanct, it is closely linked with the discharge of social responsibility. Distributive justice must be maintained *in all states of the economy*, at a given point of time and over time. These conditions also fix the maximal rate of economic growth. The Islamic point of view on growth is conditioned by two closely related considerations: (i) the general Islamic requirement to ensure a fair distribution of income and wealth *now* sets an upper bound on feasible growth rates; but (ii) the need to maintain inter-generational equity, including an explicit concern for environmental degradation, puts an upper limit on the magnitude of the resources which can be used now rather than in the future – a consideration which may justify tolerating some inequalities of income and wealth today if a more equal distribution will lower welfare tomorrow. Hence, enough resources must be spared from present use to help capital formation. However, capital formation in an Islamic economy will include human capital formation as well, thereby accentuating the emphasis on education and health. Under appropriate conditions, education will set in motion an income-equalizing mechanism of great force. That some such approach is required to satisfy the dictates of human freedom and social justice should be obvious if it is remembered that, for a vast majority of the population, the only way to earn an income is to get some employment – which, according to the credentialist view, depends on the level of educational attainment. True, the unemployed also can be paid out of the social security funds where they exist; but this is not enough because employment is also a title to self-respect in addition to being a source of income.

It may be argued that there is nothing new or distinctive about these objectives since they are common to all economic systems. One may ask if, with these common objectives, the Islamic economic system, in terms of the quality of life that it promotes, would not be similar to other economic systems. The answer is that it does not matter. The point emphasized here is that the pursuit of these objectives in an Islamic economic system must be guided and constrained by Islam's ethical philosophy. That should make a significant difference in the end result. For example, the very concepts of individual freedom, social welfare, and social responsibility have distinctive connotations in Islam and define social justice differently. Furthermore, once the requirements of social justice are specified – and resources are allocated optimally to meet them – a distinctive growth path satisfying the Islamic ethical constraints will also be determined. And something more; based on the Responsibility axiom, there will be a corrective mechanism to restore social justice in a growing economy.

NOTES

1 It may be recalled from the discussion in Chapter 2 that an additional attractive feature of Islamic economics is that its basic ethical postulates (axioms) are amenable to sensory confirmation in a real-life Muslim society. It is interesting to note that much of positive economics will fail this test of the verifiability of the basic postulates of economic theory. Indeed, Friedman (1953) explicitly excludes the basic postulates from the test of empirical verification and lays down that the validity of specific economic theories is established not by demonstrating the 'realism' of its basic postulates but by the accuracy of its predictions.

2 The absolute autonomy of man, according to Kant, is realized when he himself chooses the guiding principles of action as the most adequate expression of his being a free and rational person. See Murphy (1970).

3 According to the contractarian tradition of Rousseau and Kant,

SETTING THE POLICY OBJECTIVES

freedom lies in the observance of moral laws. For instance, Rousseau (1968) observed: '... obedience to law one prescribes to oneself is freedom' (Book 1, Chapter 8). Islam would broadly concur with such a formulation. See also the relevant discussion in Chapter 3 of this book.

4. See Nozick (1974) for a powerful advocacy of the non-consequentalist moral-rights theory.
5. See, T. H. Marshall (1950) for this point of view.
6. The Quran commends those 'Who when they spend are neither extravagant nor niggardly, but keep the golden mean' (25:67).
7. The Quran states 'Hast thou observed him who believeth religion? That is he who repelleth the orphan, And urgeth not the feeding of the needy...' (107:1–3).
8. It is interesting to note that the word 'justice' is the third-most used word in the Quran, and has been repeated more than one thousand times. (The other two words are 'Allah' and 'knowledge', in that order). It may be noted that the concept of distributive justice is a sub-set of the broader concept of 'social justice' that covers all kinds of relationships in the society; and is concerned mainly with the *economic* relationships.
9. The definitions of the equality of opportunity and the equality of result given in the text are as given in Coleman (1989).
10. The Quran says: '... those who have more do not give of their means to their captives (and thralls) so that they (may not) become their equals. Will they deny then God's beneficence?' (16:71). Two points are clear from this verse: (a) the rich must return what in their riches actually belongs to the poor; and (b) those who do not do so for fear that all will become equal in income (or consumption) are in fact being ungrateful to God.
11. The statement in the text should not be taken as implicit pleading for the labour theory of value or the marginal productivity theory, both of which suffer from severe theoretical problems.
12. The relevant verses in the Quran are: 'So that it (i.e., wealth) does not concentrate in the hands of those who are rich among you' (59:7); and 'in whose wealth a due share is included for the needy and those dispossessed' (70:24–25).
13. 'Allah's is the heritage of the heavens and the earth' (3:180), and 'spend of that whereof He [God] hath made you trustees' (57:7).
14. This, however, does not necessarily entail a reduction in the individual's right to own private property. Within the Islamic Law, the ownership right is absolute. See Taleghani (1982).
15. The Quran states: 'That which they hoard will be their collar on the Day of Resurrection' (3:180); nor is he allowed to spend it wastefully: 'Squander not your wealth among yourselves in vanity...' (4:29)].
16. The Islamic point of view is different from the Benthamite principle, which does not 'grade' happiness because, from an ethical angle, the quantity of pleasure derivable from different actions is *not* equal.

For a brief account of the Benthamite ideas, see Harrison (1989). See also footnote 20 of Chapter 5.

17 'Say (unto them, O Muhammad): Are those who know equal with those who know not? But only men of understanding will pay heed' (39:9). Note this vital point: whereas Islam seeks to equalize men (and women) with respect to their possession of income and wealth; it differentiates between them on the basis of knowledge.

18 Russell (1977) notes: 'Whenever class distinctions exist, education necessarily has two correlative defects: that of producing arrogance in the rich and that of aiming at irrational humility in the poor' (p. 86).

19 Islam also extends man's time horizon upto and beyond the Day of Judgement. This consideration alone modifies the flow and composition of the consumption goods demanded in the Islamic society. Mathematically, however, this consideration should pose no problems since, in this case, time is equated to infinity, which is the standard format of a functional with an infinite time horizon.

20 The literature on limits-to-growth – initiated by Mishan (1967) – cautioned during the 1960s against such external diseconomies of 'helter-skelter' growth. However, by the Seventies this literature ran out of steam due to a worldwide recession which raised unemployment to record levels.

21 This nonchalance towards the unemployment problem explains both the very high levels of unemployment and also their tolerance in Western economies.

22 However, in times of distress, employment may have to be created by a public works programme.

23 But no technological breakthrough can be achieved in countries with very low literacy rates; which reinforces the point, made above, that the acquisition of knowledge must be a high priority matter for an Islamic economy.

8

A TAXONOMY OF POLICY INSTRUMENTS

We now come to a discussion of the policies available to the Islamic economy to attain the pre-assigned objectives. However, there are some conceptual difficulties. First, situations will arise where the taxonomic equation between the policy objectives and the policy instruments may not be satisfied.[1] In such cases, new policy instruments will be needed to replace the ones discarded. Thus, the set of policy instruments, in certain cases, may be smaller than, say, in a capitalistic economy – e.g., while the rate of profit can be manipulated in both the economies to regulate the rate of investment, the Islamic economy will not be able to use *riba* for this or any other reason. Furthermore, excessive profits and, according to some, even land rents are also held *riba*-like.[2] The same holds for transactions like gambling, betting, and speculative transactions in the commodities, all of which have been declared *haram* (completely prohibited).

Second, replacing one policy instrument with another is not always neutral with respect to its effects on the economy. Thus, if with the abolition of interest all fixed-return instruments are replaced by only variable return instruments, the values of the key real and monetary variables may not remain the same. In particular, there may be situations when such a substitution may lead to adverse effects on the distribution of income and wealth.[3] One basic task in this area is, therefore, to find 'equivalent' policies.

Third, the question of the rate of return attached to a policy instrument may have to be interpreted in a broad way. In general, the requirement of Islamic legitimacy may have to be redefined in the context of the policy instruments available in a modern economy. The important thing is to achieve the basic objectives. It is an accepted principle of *ijtihad* that when production and social relations change dramatically with the passage of time, the question of the legitimacy of the relevant provision of the Islamic Law may have to be re-examined. Thus *if*, for instance, it can be shown that the Profit-and-Loss sharing system – duly approved by the Islamic Law – leads to an exploitative pattern of production and distribution relationships in a specific context, then either this rule should be redefined or replaced by another suitable rule (see Ch. 10). This observation implies that the concept of *riba* is not necessarily associated entirely with the fixity of the rate of return on specific policy instruments but with their exploitative implications.

To discuss the matter comprehensively, in this chapter we first take up specific policy issues, all of which relate to the real sector of the economy. The financial policies, including the problems relating to the abolition of *riba*, will be taken up in the next three chapters.

SOME KEY POLICY ISSUES

The basic principle behind the choice of policy instruments is that to reflect the Islamic ethical perception, distributive justice must hold *in all states of the economy*. As noted above, an integral part of this perception is the principle that the welfare of the least-privileged members of the society must be maximized, while their numbers are reduced to the smallest number possible. With these requirements in view, steps should be taken to correct the structure of property (especially landed property) rights, to institute a comprehensive social security system, and to institute appropriate growth-promoting policies. As these policies are put in place, the scope and form of state intervention will also have to be determined.

We now consider each of these policies in some detail.

(i) The Institution of Private Property

To achieve distributive justice in the real sense of the term, it is essential that the institution of private property is rationalized accordingly. The basic point is that, in general, Islam recognizes private property rights when acquired through one's own labour; but it has a reservation with respect to the right of an individual to hold that which is *not* due to his labour and, with respect to landed property, which he does *not* cultivate himself. According to an influential view, work is the sole basis of private property holding, and that the fact of cultivation is the only justification for the private ownership of land, which *as a rule* should be in public ownership.[4] One implication of this principle is that private holdings of land not being self-cultivated are not allowed in Islam. In general, every situation where the interest of the non-cultivators gets precedence over the interest of the cultivators is against the dictates of Islamic ethics. Thus, according to this point of view, *existing feudal structures of land holdings prevalent in most Muslim countries are contrary to the letter and spirit of the Islamic Law.*[5]

This recommendation is reinforced by the fact that tenurial structures and the inequitable working of the labour and capital markets in the developing countries contribute significantly to the prevalence of poverty – e.g., cultivators with very small or unproductive land holdings are very poor [Atkinson (1989)]. Thus, in such cases, land reforms will form the basic plank of poverty-alleviation programmes.

Sometimes this clear Islamic position is made ambiguous by the purely legalistic interpretation of the Islamic Law of Inheritance to legitimize transfer of private property to the legal heirs of the owner. Thus, the present heirs are entitled to whatever they have received from their fathers, irrespective of how it was acquired by the latter. How do we then rectify past injustices?

Unfortunately, most Muslim scholars do not appear to have applied themselves to this problem – at least, not very explicitly. One should analyse this question within the context of the general question whether the Islamic position is purely *non-consequentialist*. In other words, is it the case that individuals are entitled to exercise their property rights irrespective of their social and economic consequences, and that nothing positive can be done about its adverse fallout?[6] A positive answer to this question would violate both the axioms of Equilibrium and Responsibility, and would impede efforts to bring about distributive justice in any meaningful sense of the term. Then, there is the point that while Islam assigns a central position to the individual as a basic entity in his own right, this freedom has also been circumscribed to highlight the importance of his indissoluble links with the society. It follows that in an Islamic economy the individual's right to private property cannot be unlimited, simply because such a right can be sustained only by depriving others of their rights. Furthermore, as noted earlier, man is not the absolute owner of his property; instead, he holds the right to property only as a trust.

It follows that, *à la* the Equilibrium axiom, the law of inheritance cannot be interpreted as an unlimited licence to perpetuate the existing (unjust) institution of private property rights.[7] The correctness of this statement can be easily established by reference to the fact that the present distribution of private property – especially landed property – is not acceptable in Islam. To maintain that nothing can be done about redistributing private property rights more widely in the society, so that it remains locked within certain families, would really amount to taking the logically absurd position that the existing pattern of (landed) property holdings is in accordance with the Islamic precepts! Indeed, there is a specific provision in the Law of Inheritance itself which checks the accumulation of property – that the deceased may will at most a third of his property for the non-heirs [Guillame (1954)]. In addition, wealth, including landed property, is subject to different types of taxes – *zakat*, *khums*, *ushr*, etc.

Two clarifications should be made. First, insofar as a significant part of landed property is appropriated by the state under various land reforms, such action is not sufficient by itself to solve the problem of social inequity. The land so appropriated has to be distributed among the (private) cultivators to satisfy the requirements of social justice and growth. Second, the Islamic position that all wealth belongs to God does *not* necessarily mean that it must be held by the state for Him. All it means is that *mankind as a whole* should be the beneficiary of God's bounties, which *cannot* normally be appropriated arbitrarily either by a few persons *or* by the state; whence follows that arrangements must be made to create an appropriate institutional framework to make sure that the division of ownership rights between the individual and the state and between different individuals is properly regulated.[8]

Thus, in Muslim society, explicit laws must be enacted with a view to (i) limiting the size of private property to a socially acceptable minimum, and (ii) broad-basing the ownership of total wealth. Both these measures will have the effect of activating the institution of private property as a positive element in social dynamics, and of keeping a proper balance between the individual and the organization. To this end, wealth must be more widely distributed and utilized. In this connection, land reforms are an essential policy instrument to regulate the structure of private property rights. Simultaneously, fiscal measures to siphon off private holdings to public control should also be considered as part of the Islamic policy package to rectify inequities in initial *wealth* holdings. The basic purpose of such reforms is that, while Islam does recognize the institution of private property, it does not allow this institution to degenerate into a feudal system.

(ii) Growth-Promoting Policies

Economic growth is an important objective in an Islamic economy; but the exact policy package adopted to achieve it is an important instrument, especially to achieve distributive justice inter-temporally. As is well known, economic growth can be promoted in a variety of ways, all of which may not satisfy the requirements of distributive justice. Some growth paths may lead to greater income inequalities, which may have to be tolerated if they are shown to result from the uneven nature of the growth process, or if present inequalities of income can be shown to be necessary, though not sufficient, for promoting economic growth. But this consideration cannot be taken as a blanket approval for all kinds of income and wealth inequalities which do not bear a causative relation to economic growth. For instance, the inequalities resulting from the 'rent-seeking' type activities compromise growth instead of promoting it. The same holds for the income inequalities that result from the feudal structure of land holdings. The income flowing from such activities tends to distort the production structure by emphasizing more the needs of the rich (for luxury goods), a fact that also compromises capital formation and saving. The same applies to all types of capital gains which make the wealth concentrate even *more* among the rich – rather than *less* as enjoined by the Quran.

But the Islamic sanction would apply to all those growth policies which require the creation of an *excessively* inequitable pattern of income distribution.[9] The basic point to note here is that, from the Islamic point of view, economic growth must not lead to a perverse flow of real resources from the poor to the rich; it also should not violate the requirements of inter-generational equity. Instead, the interests of both the present generation and the posterity should be kept in view. It should also be understood that distributive justice, which inevitably involves conflict situations between the 'haves' and the 'have-nots', can be best resolved in a strongly growing economy rather than in a slow-growing or stagnant economy.

Two sets of growth-promoting policies will need to be especially emphasized in Muslim society. First, insofar as technological progress depends on greater education and health – on building up human capital – such expenditure needs to be made in earnest. Second, all policies calculated to contain the environmental damage caused by economic growth will have to be implemented to establish a better balance between man and nature.

(iii) Social Security System

Because Islam insists on distributive justice in all states of the economy, an elaborate security system will be needed to achieve it.[10] In the Islamic economy, all members are entitled to a minimum level of income *irrespective of their ability to earn it*; which follows from the separability of the ability to earn from a person's entitlement to a minimum means of livelihood. In general, what people earn does not entirely belong to them; a part of it belongs to those who, for some reason (– e.g., old age, unemployment, sickness, etc.), cannot earn. While *al-Adl* insists on a 'just' balance between the consumption, production, and distribution relations in the economy, *al-Ihsan* requires that the economic policies in a society have a distinct bias in favour of the poor. In operational terms, these requirements should translate into a wide-ranging social security system to protect those who (because of old age, ill-health, and acute poverty) cannot participate in the economic process.[11] This makes eminent economic sense because free markets do not optimally operate where they do not exist, or when the poor are excluded from them because they do not have the requisite effective demand – i.e., the need for goods is not backed by sufficient purchasing power. Thus, in general, in all cases of 'entitlement failure', when economic agents are deprived of their means of livelihood, state action will be required to rectify the situation.

A social security system will also be required to transfer income directly to the poor when the growth process does not trickle down far enough. Such transfers may take the form of income or goods. In practice, an income transfer is, perhaps, better because it provides greater flexibility in repairing entitlement failure in an exchange economy. As for financing such an elaborate social security programme, Islam does not put any restrictions on the kind of taxes levied, or on their rates. True, there are certain specific types of taxes in Islam – e.g., *zakat*, *ushr*, *khums*, etc. – but where these taxes do not raise enough revenue, or when a Muslim prefers to pay his 'dues' directly to the poor instead of paying them to the state, it will become necessary for the state to levy additional taxes. The point to remember is that while in capitalistic economies social security is a subsidiary institution, it constitutes the *first charge* on national resources in the Islamic economy.[12]

(iv) The Question of Public Ownership

As noted above, the system of free markets is not sufficient, nor even necessary, to optimize social production or consumption. Market imperfections (i.e., monopolies, externalities, etc.) drive a wedge between market profitability and social profitability of investment. Hence, state intervention is deemed warranted to attain the social optimum. The argument does not necessarily imply a complete socialization since it says nothing about the *form* such an intervention would take. At a deeper philosophical level, the question of public ownership is related to the society's general attitude towards the institution of private property. Under socialism, the right of private property is denied as all productive resources are owned by the state. Contrarily, *laissez-faire* capitalism accepts the individual's right to property as an article of faith. What is the Islamic attitude in this regard? As noted in the previous section (see footnote 10), the Quranic verse 'Unto Allah [belongeth] whatsoever is in the heavens and whatsoever is in the earth' (2:284) does not necessarily dictate complete state control of all the means of production; for, according to the Islamic philosophy, man in *his individual capacity* is God's trustee on earth.

In general, an Islamic economy will use direct and indirect controls, hopefully more of the latter type, to regulate the level and composition of production and consumption. Exactly in what proportion these controls will be combined can be decided only at the level of practical policy-making, with an inevitable element of improvisation and *ad hoc*ism. However, it is certain that the state will have to play a very important role in the Islamic economy. Excessive trust in the efficiency of the Invisible Hand (i.e., market forces) is not a part of the Islamic perspective.

However, the Islamic position on the scope of the public ownership of resources is quite clear. All natural resources – including land, natural springs, forests, oceans, water resources, mines, etc. – belong to the society as whole, and the Islamic state must distribute these resources in accordance with the Islamic law.[13] Land is in this category, and especially that which is not being cultivated – or that which is not cultivable – also belongs to the state. The individual's right to own land is, therefore, tied to the fact of cultivation; and to that extent he also has the right to dispose of it.

Apart from the public ownership of resources, the Islamic state must also be given the power to regulate economic activity and impose taxes. The basic principle is that, with respect to the ownership of land and other sources, the primary unit is the individual. The state enters as a regulator of economic activity, *not primarily as an owner*. And while Islam does not impose stringent restrictions on private ownership, it does so on spending the income from private property. State intervention *per se* is not an indicator of the supreme social good; nor is a system of free markets a guarantor of individual freedom. It is the combination of state control and free enterprise which will be used to maximize social welfare. In what proportion these arrangements are combined will depend on the purpose it is designed to serve. The ultimate objective is, once again, to ensure economic growth with distributive justice. However, it is obvious that free markets will not yield an optimal solution when a structural change involving a redistribution of private property is required. The same result holds in all such cases where the relevant markets do not exist [see Arrow (1979)].

SUMMARY

An important aspect of the problem relating to the choice of policy instruments in the Islamic economy is the need to satisfy the taxonomic equation, there being as many policy instruments as there are policy objectives. A satisfactory solution would be one where distributive justice is ensured in all states of the economy, both statically and inter-temporally. To achieve such a solution, enough policy instruments should be available to the policy-makers to redress the inequalities in the 'initial' conditions – especially with respect to those which are related to the structure of private property rights. Indeed, it can be stated unequivocally that economic growth *cannot* be equalizing if large inequalities exist in the basic structure of private property, especially landed property. Thus, it is of utmost importance that such inequities are removed through purposeful state action, especially by abolishing the feudal system. Similarly, if economic growth promotes inequities, which to some extent it does, then an elaborate social security system must be used to alleviate growth-related hardships. And the state must actively *complement*, not supplant, the market forces to ensure that individual initiative does not degenerate into a private greed for (non-productive) gains.

NOTES

1 It is a well-known principle in economics that in a general-equilibrium framework, policy instruments must be equal to the policy objectives. See, for instance, Tinbergen (1958), and Meade (1955). This is the so-called 'taxonomic' approach.
2 See Rahman (1964) and Haque (1985) for a discussion of the relevant literature.
3 For a rigorous demonstration of this point, see Naqvi and Qadir (1986).
4 The Quran says: '... man hath only that for which he maketh effort' (53:39).
5 Taleghani (1982) emphatically states: 'an extortionist feudal pattern of ownership in Islamic countries finds no support in Islamic ordinances and the laws derived from them' (p. 37). Sadr (1982) holds a similar position when he says: 'It would, therefore, be injustice to equalize the hands that had worked and toiled with the others which had not worked on the land nor toiled over it' (p. 128). However, it should be noted that there are others who hold that

the leasing of land for cultivation is allowed in Islam. For details of this controversy, see Haque (1977).
6 Such a non-consequentialist, purely procedural (moral), theory of entitlements has been proposed by Nozick (1974). This theory allows no 'patterning' of the existing distribution of private property on any grounds whatsoever. See Chapter 6 of the present book for more discussion on this point.
7 Taleghani (1982) has highlighted the limited nature of private property rights in Islam by reference to an important implication of the Islamic Law of Inheritance, which is that it *restricts the ownership of wealth only to the life-time of the owners*; they have no right to make a will which contravenes the law. Kahf (1978) also makes the same point.
8 It may be recalled that Abu Dharr had vigorously protested against Mu'awiya's efforts (651 A.D) to change the nomenclature of *mal-al-Muslimin* (wealth of the Muslims) to *mal-al-Allah* (wealth of God). Abu Dharr saw in this move a clever plan to appropriate private wealth to fulfil the ruler's ambitions. See Haque (1977) on this point. The implication of Abu Dharr's position in modern times is that the answer to the problem of private-enterprise-capitalism is *not* state-capitalism. The Islamic position rejects both these positions as they are contrary to the Equilibrium axiom. Giving a sense of participation to the common man in the working of socio-economic institutions, through an effective *decentralization of the ownership positions*, is an integral part of Islam's economic philosophy.
9 Such a policy was followed in Pakistan, as in many other developing countries, during the Sixties. It led to a large accumulation of (investible) capital and profits while the real wages did not rise in tandem. The import substitution process also helped profits to rise even more by *creating* domestic monopolies in the domestic production of such goods. While this policy definitely helped capital formation in the large-scale manufacturing sector, it also created a significant idle industrial capacity. As predicted by economic theory, the monopolist producers maximized their profits without any pressure to raise output as well. Furthermore, this policy imposed a substantial consumption cost on the society by substituting low-quality and high-priced domestically produced import substitutes for the relatively low priced high-quality imported goods. Such a policy also had the effect of worsening income distribution between labour and capital. For a detailed discussion of Pakistan's growth strategy during this period, see Naqvi (1971).
10 An elaborate social security has been used in the West, especially in Germany, where Bismark introduced it in 1896 to help the elderly, *because* the households will not save enough on their own for old age, and *because* private markets will not provide certain types of insurance due to problems of adverse selection. See Kotlikoff (1989).
11 For an elaboration of this point, see Shafi (1968) and Naqvi et al. (1977, 1978).

A TAXONOMY OF POLICY INSTRUMENTS

12 Thus, unlike the capitalistic societies, including the welfare state, an Islamic state will cut social security payment only as the *last* resort.
13 For a detailed discussion, see Taleghani (1982). There is a universal agreement in Muslim scholarship on this point.

9
THE PROBLEM OF ABOLISHING INTEREST: I

In this and the next two chapters, we propose to consider the problem of replacing *riba* in an Islamic economy. This is one of the most important and yet the most difficult issues of Islamic economics; important, because the injunction against *riba* signifies a distinctive socio-economic philosophy which abhors social exploitation in all forms, including 'unbalanced' and iniquitous financial relationships; difficult, because its abolition – and replacement by an alternative system – calls for innovative, ethically acceptable, and efficient policy initiatives. In particular, any alternative system must ensure that adequate provision is made, *in all states of the economy*, to safeguard the economic interests of the least-privileged in the society, of whom a common characteristic is that they are risk-averters. Two negative statements follow from this basic consideration. First, any formulation that concentrates *only* on some formal aspects of the problem of replacing *riba* in an Islamic economy – e.g., *completely* replacing the policy instruments that bear fixed rates of return by those that promise *only* variable rates of return – really trivializes the problem and its solution. Second, it will be naive to think that a 'replacement' of one financial instrument by another will be neutral with respect to the effects of such 'reform' on the key real variables of the economy.

In view of the great complexity of the problem, we first clarify the meaning of the Islamic injunction against *riba*, and then go on to consider, in Chapter 10, the economic and ethical credentials of some popular proposals, especially those which seek to replace *riba* by some latter-day variant of the profit-and-loss sharing principle. In Chapter 11, we lay down the elements of a non-trivial solution of the problem. The basic motivation of these chapters is that finding a viable alternative for *riba* in a modern economy is no simple matter; and what solutions may have been adequate in the simple economies of the middle ages are probably unsatisfactory to-day. Indeed, a radical change in the relations of production and in the associated financial structure necessitates a re-examination of the legitimacy of specific policies even from a purely theological point of view.

A FEW CLARIFICATIONS

Insofar as the Islamic injunction against *riba* means abolishing of *interest* in the modern sense of the term, a few remarks are in order to clarify the true import of the Islamic injunction.[1]

Firstly, the proposal to abolish interest is a key element of the set of Islamic policy instruments, *not* a policy objective. The objective is to find a solution which is consistent with the dictates of the Islamic ethical axioms.

Secondly, while a zero rate of interest may be a necessary condition, it is by no means sufficient to 'span' an Islamic economy. This statement can be proved by considering that while the existence of an Islamic economy implies a zero rate of interest, the reverse does not *necessarily* hold. This observation has two clear logical implications: (i) a zero rate of interest occurs whenever an Islamic economy exists, and (ii) it is possible that a zero rate of interest occurs even without the existence of an Islamic economy.[2] Put together, these two statements suggest that a zero rate of interest is not *sufficient* to prove the existence of an Islamic economy.[3]

Thirdly, the Islamic reform is not just a question of replacing interest by *some* financial instruments promising variable rates of return, or by those which involve risk and uncertainty. The more substantive part of the solution of the problem is to devise financial instruments which combine the Islamic ethical concern for the low-income risk-averse investor with the requirements of financial efficiency. Indeed, a mere formalistic and cosmetic change that does not reflect such concerns may not qualify as Islamic reform, even if it is legally permissible. *To replace interest by profit is not necessarily an Islamic reform either, because it might replace capitalism based on interest-and-profit by a capitalism which is based only on profit!*[4]

Fourthly, the validity of the statement that the abolition of interest *by itself* will lead to the realization of the objectives of the Islamic economy (e.g., the equity objective) is highly suspect. In fact, it can be argued that such a step, depending on the character of the financial mechanism that replaces interest, may as much cause a 'divergent' movement leading away from the goal of an Islamic economic system as one towards it. The divergent movement – that results in raising the level of exploitation in the society – will occur if some financial reforms force all classes of savers (investors) to take a risk – out of all proportion to their ability to do so.[5] In this case, the small investors will be crowded out of the financial market.[6] Such a reform, even if it qualifies to be Islamic in a formal sense, will definitely not be an acceptable alternative to interest.

Fifthly, granting that the focus of Islamic reform is not so much on *abolishing* interest as on *replacing* it by a legitimate financial mechanism, the Islamic injunction need not necessarily negate the Fisherian explanation for the 'existence' of a positive rate of interest, viz., the net productivity of the 'roundabout' methods of production and a positive preference for present consumption over future consumption.[7] It is only that Islam does not accept it as a *justification* for perpetuating the *institution* of interest. The Islamic injunction against interest is, in fact, a special case of a more general rule which prohibits *all* financial deals that perpetuate, or create, distributional inequalities.

Sixthly, it should be understood clearly that a zero rate of interest in the context of the Islamic economy does not necessarily denote a state of capital saturation, although this possibility is not excluded from consideration.[8] The injunction against interest holds in conditions of capital scarcity as well. This observation should make it absolutely clear that the Islamic commandment *to abolish* riba *in no way implies that, as a general rule, capital will have a zero 'shadow' price in an Islamic economy.*

Finally, contrary to a popular misconception, a positive interest rate does *not* always mean a policy instrument promising a risk-free (fixed) rate of return. It all depends on the *assumptions* made about the economic universe: the rate of return will be a fixed amount if perfect certainty is assumed; it will be a risk-free rate *plus* a risk-premium (which is variable) term if economic decisions are made under conditions of uncertainty. [Ingram (1989)]. Yet another relevant consideration is that there is no such thing as *the* rate of interest; but it is only a term structure of interest rates. Thus, when we refer to the fixity of the rate of interest, it is the *average* of (many) rates of interest prevailing in the market that we talk about, not the *individual* interest rates, which *may* (and do) vary.

AN ISLAMIC PERSPECTIVE ON INTEREST

The present section seeks to determine a 'policy equivalent' of interest – i.e., a policy, or a set of policies, which makes the same impact on the economy as does interest. This is done by identifying the *functions* performed by interest in a modern economy, and then by determining the Islamic point of view about each one of them. This procedure will also enable us to find a set of rules that help a 'stylized' (Islamic) economy grow at the optimal rate and also satisfy Islamic ethical concerns in an inter-temporal context.[9]

To this end, we make use of the celebrated result that a positive interest is (mathematically) 'separable' from the functions that it performs. The procedure is to maximize a current-value utility functional, subject to the constraints of technology and the restrictions on the initial conditions relating to the size of the existing level of capital stock.[10] The utility functional can be readily interpreted as also incorporating the requirements of the risk-averse investor. The problem is solved by manipulating the values of the control variable (per capita consumption in our case) so that the growth rate of the economy and the allocation of investment between generations are determined together.

It can be shown that interest in a dynamic real economy (i.e., with no money in it) is equal to the net marginal productivity of capital. This equation, in turn, yields four distinct though additive functions:

(i) to offset the (adverse) effects of a positive social rate of time preference on savings and investment;
(ii) to compensate for the secular decline in the marginal utility of saving owing to its growth;
(iii) to provide for the physical depreciation of the country's capital stock; and,
(iv) when money is introduced into the system, to allow

for the effects of changing price expectations on the real value of savings and investment.

It is important to note that the ensuing analysis is restricted to steady-state (i.e., long-run equilibrium) situations under conditions of certainty. Of course, in real-life situations, off-the-steady-state behaviour, under conditions of uncertainty, should be more interesting. As noted below, for disequilibrium situations, *new* investment will also appear as one of the terms in the equation.

According to most Muslim economists, an element of uncertainty must be allowed for to gain legitimacy in financial transactions. But this must be qualified because any uncertain individual situation can be converted into an 'as-if certain' average situation by making an explicit provision for an appropriate risk premium to hedge against uncertainty. As in quantum mechanics, in economics, too, there is no guarantee about the individual outcome, but we are pretty sure of the average outcome.[11]

(i) The Problem of Positive Time Preference

It should be obvious that the positivity of the rate of time preference, reflecting the essentially myopic nature of the individual's economic calculus, should be acceptable in Islam.[12] This is because a zero time preference will impose too heavy a consumption sacrifice on the present generation for the sake of the posterity. The real question, therefore, is: how high will be the rate of time preference in an Islamic economy? The answer is that it will probably be low. This is because a positive time preference derives its plausibility from the hard economic fact that while the present income can be deployed to take advantage of profitable investment opportunities in the future (so long as the marginal productivity is positive and large), the income accruing in the future cannot be so used to benefit from the opportunities available in the present. Then, in order to have the individual's preferences reflected into collective decisions, the government must find a way of averaging them.[13] But this exercise will require positing axioms based on an irreducible value judgement with respect to the ethical biases of a given society. This is because, for purposes of averaging, relative 'weights' must be assigned to individual preferences. But it may be noted that, by virtue of Arrow's Paradox of Majority Voting, democratic procedures by themselves do not supply an infallible rule to force consistency between the choices made by a group, and the individual choices in that group.[14]

The important question is: how can the task of turning a positive time preference to negative be accomplished in the Islamic society?[15] More simply, how to generate positive savings in the face of positive (though much lower) time preference, with the rate of interest at zero? The key to an understanding of the problem lies in the 'fact' that while *private* time preference will continue to be positive, there is no need for *public* time preference also to remain positive. Thus, generating 'net' saving really amounts to *more than* offsetting the private positive time preference by a government time preference that is *negative*.

(ii) The Marginal Utility (Disutility) of Consumption (Savings) over Time

The other two functions relate to replacing the capital used up in the process of economic growth; to the obvious fact that the marginal utility of consumption rises as total savings get bigger over time; and to the expectation that the investor's future income may be enhanced by a favourable technological change. It should be clear that the utility of consumption remains positive over time because per capita consumption must also be positive. On the contrary, a sufficiently high rate of per capita consumption guarantees a positive utility of consumption.[16] That being the case, we reach the obvious conclusion that as the rate of economic growth is accelerated, government policy in the Islamic economy must aim at raising per capita consumption, especially of the least-privileged in the society.

(iii) The Depreciation of Capital and New Investment

An explicit provision will have to be made in the Islamic economy for the depreciating capital stock in a dynamic equilibrium; and to allow for new investment as well when the economy is out of equilibrium. In all probability, the financing will come largely from public savings. But that does not necessarily mean that private savings will be elbowed out, and that the government will be making all the investment decisions. Indeed, if individuals do not squander wealth in deference to the clear-cut Islamic injunction, private savings may even rise. The point is that savings should be large enough to finance capital depreciation.

(iv) Introducing Money

If money is introduced into the system, then we are dealing essentially with a two-goods economy instead of a one-good economy that we have assumed so far. In such an economy, a simple way of dealing with the problem is to assume that the shadow (relative) price of capital is also the market price of capital. This is a reasonable assumption because, in steady-state (equilibrium) situations, there will be no distortion in the system – i.e., the marginal rate of substitution (in a closed economy) will be equal to the marginal rate of transformation. Once that is done, we have to analyse not only the effects of a change in the relative prices but also in the absolute price level; and to allow for the possibility of inflation.[17]

We have noted above that steps will have to be taken to safeguard the real value of private savings, and to provide reserve funds to finance the escalation of the monetary expenditure on depreciation and new investment.[18] This does not pose any problem so long as the tax-base is price-elastic, so that the tax revenue increases automatically in periods of inflation. The first problem must be tackled, however, in a more systematic fashion. It appears that a system of linking private savings with an appropriate cost-of-living index may provide an answer – perhaps the only answer – to this problem.[19] It is true that, under certain conditions, this may build an inflationary bias into the economy; but the problem has to be faced. To this end, a system of 'imperfect indexing' will have to be devised in which the Central Bank partially offsets the decline in the real value of private savings caused by inflation. This will take care of the problem of the inflationary bias also. (More on this in Chapter 11).

SUMMARY

The argument so far can be easily summarized. Abolishing *riba*, if interpreted as interest in the modern sense of the term, is really about *replacing riba* by a set of policy instruments which perform the same functions presumably more efficiently *and* equitably. A binding constraint on the solution set is that the Islamic ethical concerns must be met. There are two elements of this constraint: firstly, the distribution of income and wealth must not worsen *as a result of* the Islamic reform; secondly, the financial arrangements replacing interest should not crowd out the small, risk-averse investor. In other words, finding an Islamic solution means being mindful of its economic consequences; of such changes in the real and the financial sectors of the economy as are caused by the abolition of *riba*. This is the meaning of our basic thesis that the Islamic solution should be non-trivial. An example of a trivial solution is to 'reform' the existing interest-and-profit-based (capitalistic) system with one that is *only* profit-based. Depending on the institutional context, such a reform is as likely to raise as to lower the overall level of exploitation in the economy. The acceptability, from the Islamic point of view, will have to be decided on a case-by-case basis. Some of these issues are examined in greater detail in the next chapter.

NOTES

1 Nearly all English translations of the Quran translate *riba* as usury. See Abdullah Yusuf Ali (1938), who interprets *riba* (usury) as the opposite extreme of 'charity, unselfishness, striving and giving of ourselves in the service of God and of our follow-men.' Thus, 'my definition [of *riba*] would include profiteering of all kinds, but exclude economic credit, the creature of modern banking and finance.' According to one section of Islamic opinion, *riba* stands for all kinds of interest, simple or compound. In Pakistan, the Shariat Court has taken this view. Yet there are some who insist that *riba* means only usury (or compound interest) [Rahman (1964)]. According to yet another opinion, *riba* includes a lot more than just interest – e.g., all unearned income taking the form of interest, usury, and land rent which accrues to owners without equivalent exchange. Thus, Ibn al-Arabi (1957) distinguished 56 types of *riba*. A comprehensive analysis of these contrasting opinions is given in Haque (1985). However, to avoid unnecessary controversy, we do not go into the controversy about what constitutes *riba* [For various

interpretations of *riba*, see Khan (1991)]. Instead, we focus on *evaluating the merits of the alternative ways of pricing capital* once interest is abolished.

2 In the terse language of mathematical logic: if A (=an Islamic economic system) then B (=a zero rate of interest), does not exclude B occurring without A. Also, B if only A does not preclude B occurring without A. See Gemignani (1968).

3 This conclusion also agrees with 'commonsense' because Islam not only prohibits interest but most aleatory (*gharar*) transactions – pure speculative deals, forward trading, etc. Abolishing interest does not automatically lead to the elimination of all aleatory deals.

4 Contrary to the widespread misconception, the capitalistic system is *not exclusively interest-based*. It is rather based on interest *and* profits, with the element of profit rising as the economy becomes more prosperous, so that the average level of risk aversion declines.

5 Interest-bearing debenture is the low-yield option for risk-averters. On the other hand, the risk-takers go for higher-yielding but risky stocks. Abolishing all interest-bearing options, therefore, will amount to asking all risk-averters to become risk-takers, which is not a very reasonable thing to do – it is even unnatural.

6 In terms of the Fisherian diagram, measuring present consumption on the horizontal axis and future consumption along the vertical axis, the vertical bias, or the relative steepness, of both the production possibility frontier *and* the indifference *curve* explains the existence of a positive rate of interest. If the production possibility frontier and the consumption indifference curve were *both* made symmetrical around the 45° line, then the rate of interest will be zero. It should be clearly understood that this is *not* necessarily the assumption behind the abolition of interest in Islam. In fact, it is shown in the ensuing discussion that the individual's time preference will continue to be positive – i.e., the consumption indifference curves will have a vertical bias in an Islamic economy. However, government action should have the effect of *reversing* this bias in the individual indifference curves.

7 Koopmans (1957) points out that a state of capital saturation is perfectly consistent with a zero rate of interest. However, this 'golden age', with a zero rate of interest, may not be realizable in the real world because (i) the social time preference is excessively high so that all saving ceases at the existing (low) rate of interest; and (ii) the profit rate, inclusive of the premium for risk, reaches a ceiling to prevent any *additional investment from occurring before the interest rate is pushed down to zero*.

8 A full mathematical demonstration of the assertion made in this section is given in Naqvi (1981), and Naqvi and Qadir (1986).

9 A *functional* is to be distinguished from a *function*. Given a function (or curve) a functional yields another function. For a clear exposition of this concept, see Pontryagin *et al.* (1962).

10 See Naqvi and Qadir (1986). Chapter 3.

11 However, if time preference is negative, then saving will be positive

even with a zero rate of interest. By the same token, a neutral time preference, with a zero rate of interest, will entail a zero marginal rate of saving. However, it should be noted that a few empirical studies by Modigliani, Brumberg, and others have shown that the marginal rate of saving may not be related directly to changes in the rate of change in interest rates.

12 According to the classical Ramsey (1928) – Pigou (1962) argument, it is not morally right for the government to entertain a positive time preference because, unlike individuals, it is *not* myopic. On the other hand, as Marglin (1963) has argued, it is undemocratic for governments not to discount the future while individuals do the discounting, since democratic governments must reflect the preferences of the individuals in a given society.

13 Arrow (1951) shows, for example, that the transitivity axiom, which is valid for individual preference orderings, may be violated in the case of a group ranking based on majority voting.

14 This is exactly what a positive rate of interest does in a capitalistic economy to generate positive saving: in effect, it turns a positive time preference to negative. Alternatively, one can also think of a positive rate of interest as enhancing the future income of the savers by making it possible to lend the present income for future consumption. In the case noted in the text, a positive rate of interest plays the role of *decreasing* the amounts of future income, which can be transferred to present consumption through borrowing.

15 A proof of this statement is a non-trivial exercise. It rests on the proposition that the utility of consumption is a unique function of time for a given initial utility, and of the rate of growth of per capita consumption. See Naqvi and Qadir (1986), pp. 50–53.

16 A widely accepted result is that inflation tends to reduce optimal per capita consumption below the level indicated by the Golden Rule of Accumulation. [See Jovanovic, (1982)]. This is because inflation increases the cost of holding money-balances.

17 As shown in Naqvi and Qadir (1986), the introduction of money into the system essentially does not modify the analysis in the real-economy context.

18 When it is remembered that, in periods of rapid inflation, the interest rate often becomes negative in real terms, the policy proposed in the text should be seen as producing better results in terms of its effects on the generation of savings. An alternative proposal is discussed in Chapter 11.

10

THE PROBLEM OF ABOLISHING INTEREST: II

The preceding chapter outlined the nature and dimension of the problem of replacing *riba*, understood as interest, as a policy instrument in an Islamic economy. The next to examine is the viability of the policies that could replace interest efficiently *and* equitably. To begin with, we focus in the present chapter on those instruments which *do not* constitute an appropriate solution of the problem.

(i) Can Interest be Abolished by Administrative *Fiat*?

It has often been asserted at the level of popular discourse that interest should be abolished with one stroke of the pen. But this is not a solution, because if interest is *abolished* instead of being *replaced* – on the understanding that capital has a zero price – then all capital will depreciate without replacement through unrestricted capital consumption. This result can be proved by showing that the utility of per capita consumption increases over time exponentially if the interest rate is set equal to zero. That this in fact is the case can be easily understood if it is remembered that abolishing the interest rate by an administrative *fiat* will lead to a maximal marginal utility of *consumption*, which is another way of saying that the marginal utility of saving (investment) will be minimal.[1] Setting the interest rate equal to zero means that the price of capital is arbitrarily put below this lower limit. This puts a premium on present consumption as opposed to future consumption (i.e., savings). Thus, the utility of per capita consumption increases exponentially over time.

Fortunately, the majority of Muslim economists agree that the focus of Islamic reform is not on *abolishing* interest – i.e., by setting the price of capital equal to zero; it is rather on *replacing* it by an alternative mechanism of determining the rate of return on capital. However, it is not unusual to find the (correct) statement that an administrative *fiat* will be involved in devising any alternative to the present system confused with the (wrong) statement that *all it takes* to introduce Islamic reform is to abolish interest by an administrative *fiat* [for instance, Siddiqi (1983)].

(ii) PLS, Equities, and Bonds

The most widely advocated financial arrangement – in place of the interest-based transaction – is the one based on the Profit-and-Loss (PLS)-sharing (*Mudarabah*) principle.[2]

This principle is held to be legitimate presumably because of its two basic characteristics: (i) according to it, the two parties to the bargain must get a 'fair' share in total profits in a *proportion* mutually and voluntarily agreed upon in *advance*; (ii) such financial dealings facilitate transactions in goods and services, and not just in those involving money only. In contrast, the interest-based transactions *do not* possess these characteristics partly because they insist on a fixed rate of return (i.e., rental) on capital, which is not necessarily a function of the profits made in a given transaction; and partly because such interest-based financial transactions are not typically related to any 'real' economic activity – e.g., the various types of speculative deals. Comparing these two types of financial arrangements, the PLS-type is *assumed* to be both efficient and just – efficient, because such transactions increase the level of financial intermediation, relating the real and financial sectors of the economy in a fruitful and complementary fashion; and just, because monetary rewards flowing from such activities are distributed *equitably* (not necessarily equally) between the lender and the borrower of capital.[3]

An important difference between the interest-based and the PLS-type of financial arrangements has to do with the degree of variability of, and the uncertainty about, the size of the rental on capital. The interest-based transactions are usually seen as those where, given the rate of interest, one can expect with *certainty* what the (absolute) size of the return on capital would be. By contrast, in the PLS-type financial instruments the rental on capital, in absolute terms, can be positive, zero, or negative; and the monetary authority is *not* supposed to intervene to guarantee a given (positive) rate of return.

In the traditional treatment of the problem, somehow the variability of the rate of return – and its being risky – gets the most prominence, although this may not always be the case. True, the PLS-type financial instruments (e.g., equities) are more variable than the fixed-return financial instruments (e.g., bonds) – i.e., the standard deviation around the average is significantly larger for the former type than for the latter type.[4] But it is not correct to maintain that the rate of return on the latter type is completely fixed. Indeed, in some respects, the rates of return on both types are variable; and to some extent both are fixed. Both are variable when, like the PLS, the rate of interest varies during the course of, say, a calender year, and a person investing for short periods, say for three months at a time, may see the rate of interest changed on the same financial instrument. But both are fixed to the extent that, like the interest rate, the rate of profit on the PLS instruments is also fixed in advance. Furthermore, any PLS-(variable return) instrument has an element of fixity to the extent that the government is willing to guarantee a certain (expected) rate of return.[5] And, as noted in Chapter 10, like the profit rate (which is defined as interest *plus* a stochastic term), the interest rate in an uncertain world also has an additive variable term to compensate for risk and uncertainty [Ingram (1984)].

(iii) The Fixed Rate of Return vs The Variable Rate of Return

It has been asserted that the Islamic financial reform is formally equivalent to replacing financial instruments bearing fixed rates of return by instruments promising *only* variable rates of return. However, this proposal is defective.[6] First, such an assertion is clearly fallacious: from the *correct* statement that the legitimate PLS-type financial instruments bear variable rates of return, it deduces the *wrong* conclusion that *all* financial instruments promising variable rates of return are legitimate. Second, this proposal involves making assumptions about the element of risk and uncertainty and about how much of it can be tolerated by different classes of investors (savers). Indeed, the value judgement appears to be that risk and uncertainty are a 'good' rather than a 'bad' element. Third, such a proposal (mistakenly) asserts that equity-financing is somehow 'separable' from debt-financing in a typical money market. Third, the proposal involves taking an all-or-none position about the two types of policy instruments, ignoring all intermediate combinations of the two types. A more realistic view will be to think in terms of a *spectrum* of financial instruments, with the zero-risk option and the high-risk option as the polar extremes. Fourth, the proposed reforms also assume that all or most of the people in an Islamic economy are perfect risk-takers, so that the problem of risk aversion will not arise in such an economy; which, of course, is an oversimplification, to say the least.

We will now show that most of these assertions are questionable both on the efficiency and the equity grounds.

(a) From Interest Rates to Profit Shares: It has been argued that in an Islamic economy the profit shares will do the job that the interest rate does at present.[7] It can be shown that this need not be the case. Since in an economic universe *assumed* to be characterized by perfect certainty, the profit rate differs from the interest rate by a positive stochastic factor signifying risk, there are only two possibilities. *Either* this stochastic term is zero *or* it is not zero. If it is zero – or more accurately, tends to zero – then investors, when confronted with a choice between different kinds of policy instruments, will strictly prefer those which promise a fixed rate of return. In other words, the two elements of the proposition – that the profit rates are formally equivalent to the interest rates, and that in an Islamic system the variable-returns instruments are the only ones available – cannot both hold at the same time. But when the relevant economic universe is assumed to be uncertain, the rate of interest and the rate of profit are practically equivalent; and any difference between the two is a matter of degree, not of kind: *both are variable*, though the degree of variability may be greater in the one than in the other [Bliss (1990)].

(b) The Preference for the Variable-return Instruments: It has been asserted that a general case can be made to show that, even if varying degrees of risk aversion are allowed, the variable-returns instruments will be rationally preferred even by risk-

averse investors.[8] But such a result need not hold generally. Instead, making appropriate assumptions about risk aversion, the variable-returns financial instruments can be shown to be preferred to the fixed-return instruments *if* all investors can anticipate with *complete confidence* that the former will *always* yield a greater rate of return than the latter.[9] However, if all investors, *irrespective of their capacities to take risk,* already know for sure that they will be getting a better deal investing in the variable-return instruments, than in the fixed-return instruments, then they will 'naturally' opt for the former.[10]

Such an assumption, or belief, implies that the rates of return can be predicted with complete confidence for all classes of investors; and that, in general, financial instruments with variable rates of return are the same as those promising a fixed rate of return. But, in a regime of perfect certainty, *this* does not make sense because the two types of financial instruments do differ by a risk factor. Even more importantly, this result, if true, renders totally pointless the discussion about the *superior* merits of a regime of variable-returns instruments on which the rate of return *cannot* be predicted with complete confidence.

(c) Is Equity-Financing 'Separable' from Debt-Financing?: The implementation of the Islamic profit-and-loss sharing principle is seen by some as equivalent to a substitution of equity financing for debt financing.[11] The assumption is that the modern money markets can work on the basis of equity-financing alone, with no help from debt-financing instruments (bonds). But the matter is not as simple as that. It is *not* known what will happen once debt financing is *completely* abolished. In modern money markets, the two types of instruments are *not* separable; indeed they are functionally related so that the movements in one get transmitted to the other. Furthermore, a significant part of the variations in the equities (ordinary stocks) can be explained in terms of the rate of interest and the speculative changes in the rate of return on stocks, which are totally unrelated to the developments in the real sector of the economy.[12] Only a part of the total variation is explained by the profitability of the relevant industries/firms. Obviously, insofar as the rate of return on them is explained by speculation and the market rate of interest, equities also should *not* be acceptable in Islam!

(d) Is Uncertainty per se Desirable?: It has been argued that one of the essential 'facts' of life in the Islamic economy is that it is characterized by uncertainty and risk. And, so the argument goes, it is immoral and unjust to claim a pre-determined return when the future cannot be predicted with certainty.[13] Hence, the need for devising policy instruments where the returns are uncertain (variable). The argument appears to be sound; but it must be carefully phrased to avoid the implicit value judgement that uncertainty or risk-taking are desirable *per se*. Because if it was true that the more risky the option the better it is from an *ethical* point of view, then gambling, betting, and other similar activities would not have been declared *haram* (prohibited) in Islam. Even from a purely economic point of view, if the risk is increased without bound, it would cause the investment – and in a two-factors economy, also the *wages* – to tend to zero. This is because when the risk is very high, the expected profits will have to be correspondingly high. Such a situation, in practice, would be characterized by extreme inequalities of income and wealth – crowding out of the financial market all but the very rich who can afford to take high risks – which would violate the Equilibrium axiom.[14]

Our analysis should also discredit the notions that the real world is characterized by either all-risk or no-risk situations, and that there will not be (or should not be) any serious problem of risk aversion in an Islamic economy; or that no ethical problems will arise on this score. In fact, in the real world, there is a continuum of risk aversion – and of (reciprocal) risk-taking – in which the risk should be minimized. And crucial issues of Islamic ethics do arise in cases where no attention is paid to those persons who cannot afford to take risk, or whose capacity to take risk is severely limited by their low income.

(iv) The Ethic of the PLS

It is also interesting to note that the literature reviewed above does not explicitly incorporate the main Islamic ethical concerns, not even as an after-thought to check whether an unrestricted system of profit-and-loss-sharing satisfies them. For instance, in proving that a banking system based on profit-and-loss-sharing – one that does not guarantee the nominal value of the deposits – is more 'stable', no attention is paid to the effects of such a scheme on the interests of the risk-averters, a class of people about whom Islam worries the most. Also, while it is shown that a system based on profit-and-loss-sharing in some sense will be Pareto-optimal, it is forgotten that this exclusively efficiency-oriented criterion may be totally irrelevant in an Islamic economy, where efficiency must be combined with equity no matter what.

In almost every analytical effort made so far to prove the superiority of a profit-based system over an interest-based system, an implicit assumption has been made that since profit-based arrangements are (technically) allowed by the *Shariah* (Islamic law), they must *ipso facto* be ethically right; and hence, there is no need to check the economic consequences of specific financial arrangements for consistency with Islamic ethical axioms. [Siddiqi (1983a)]. But such an (implicit) argument trivializes the problem of the choice of policy instruments, because, for this way of thinking, such choices have already been made for us. Such an argument also closes the door on *ijtihad* (legalistic interpretation) because it assumes that each and every aspect of a given (dominant) interpretation of the Islamic law is unalterable data.

In the present discussion, we do not share such (implicit or explicit) assumptions; instead we maintain that while the sanction against interest is Divine, there is all the room for a debate about the alternatives to it. That being the case, all such proposals should be subjected to a detailed analysis with a view to *falsifying* them by reference to their economic and social consequences. In case it can be shown that such text-book arrangements do not work efficiently in the real world, or that they are not consistent with the dictates of Islamic ethics, then these considerations should be taken into account by the Muslim jurists in order to revise the relevant provisions of the Islamic law.

There is another aspect of the PLS-type transactions which merits attention from the ethical point of view. Such transactions require that the loss, if any, should be borne by the lender, while the profits are shared between the lender and the borrower according to an agreed formula. Such an unequal lender-borrower relationship is based on the perception that the lender is a rich man while the borrower is the man in need – e.g., a person who has ideas but not much money. Where such a perception holds – e.g., say in a small-scale business short on capital – the PLS principle is sound; but such a perception is ill-founded where the lender is typically a small stock-holder and of relatively small means while the borrower is very rich – i.e., a large joint stock company. The fact is that the lender-borrower relationship in to-day's world is tilted in favour of the borrower; and, in all such cases, to ask only the lender to bear the entire loss would not be an ethically correct position.

What else, then, satisfies the Islamic ethic in financial arrangements? Obviously, a specific financial arrangement should be related to an Islamically just (real) transaction to satisfy the equity requirement; only then would the return on such transactions would also meet the Islamic criterion. Contrariwise, financial transactions which are highly profitable but finance unjust or socially wasteful transactions – e.g., most speculative deals would fall in this category – will not satisfy the requirements of Islamic ethic. This brings us to the fundamental point that Islamic ethic *cannot be made contingent* to the substitution of profit for interest. It has to be decided independently, and on a case by case basis. For the economy as a whole, it is essential that any financial reform based on the PLS system, or any other principle recognized by Islam, must not lead to a concentration of wealth in fewer hands, and especially to a crowding out of the financial market of the risk-averter and the small investor. But such a result *will* follow when an unrestricted PLS system makes the element of risk in financial transitions too high. [See Naqvi and Qadir (1986)]. This consideration once again brings us to the points made earlier – namely, that risk and uncertainty are inevitable elements of the economic universe, but these need to be minimized to create conditions which are conducive to investment; and, also, that there is nothing ethical about risk and uncertainty *per se*.

SUMMARY

The many arguments evaluated so far contain important elements of truth but suffer from a series of misconceptions. Most of these arguments centre on the desirability, from an Islamic ethical point of view, of profits *per se* as opposed to interest; of the variable-returns instrument as compared to the fixed-return investment; and of risk-taking and uncertainty as against a preference for non-risk and certain outcomes. Much confusion also surrounds the problem of risk aversion in the Islamic economy. There is a corresponding failure to analyse from an Islamic point of view the consequences of the fact that risk and uncertainty will have to be *minimized* in order to encourage saving and investment, prevent an undue concentration of income and wealth in a few hands (of the rich, the high risk-takers), and safeguard the interests of the relatively poor (the risk-averters). But the most fundamental deficiency of such arguments is their failure to explicitly incorporate the Islamic ethical imperatives. In these arguments, the ethical considerations are made *contingent* to the adoption of a system of profit-sharing, which is prejudged as just from an Islamic point of view. But, from a logical point of view, this is to trivialize the problem of incorporating ethics into the corpus of Islamic economics – and that too as an after-thought! Indeed, this way of thinking assumes away the real problem by narrowly defining Islamic justice.

NOTES

1 As shown in Chapter 10, the truth of these statements can be understood by remembering that a positive social rate of time preference and a positive capital depreciation require a positive price of capital; and that the sum of these two elements sets a lower limit on this price.
2 There are many other types of transactions – e.g., *Musharaka, Murabaha* – which are legitimate in Islam. But the basic principle of profit-and-loss-sharing underlines all these financial instruments in differing degrees and forms. The main contributors to this debate are Siddiqi (1983); Chapra (1985); Khan (1985); Anwar (1987).
3 According to the prototype *Mudarabah*, while the profits are shared in a ratio agreed to between the borrower and the lender of the capital *in advance*, the losses must be borne entirely by the lender of the capital. It has been noted by some Muslim scholars that, unlike *riba, Mudarabah* is *not* a Quranic concept. The latter was a pre-Islamic practice that the Prophet did not oppose. Ibn Hazm (1350 A.H.) notes that: '*Mudarabah* was practised in pre-Islamic Arabia. The tribe of Quraish had no other livelihood but trade. The old people, women, children, and orphans used to give their capital on the basis of *Mudarabah* to the merchants for a certain part of the profit' (p. 247). Thus, it is significant that the Quran contraposes *riba* (which is prohibited as being symptomatic of social exploitation) and *sadaqa* (charity, altruistic behaviour which is encouraged) but not *riba* and *Mudarabah*, which, if not more, can be

as exploitative as *riba*. See also Haque (1985) for a detailed discussion of these matters.
4 A study of the U.S. financial market over a 58-year period (1926–84) shows that the standard deviation works out to be 21.38% for stocks and 7.58% for bonds.
5 Such guarantees, in fact, have been provided in Pakistan by the Government and by the State Bank of Pakistan.
6 The discussion in the rest of this chapter is based on Naqvi (1981).
7 For instance, Siddiqi (1983).
8 See Khan (1985).
9 This result is formally proved in Naqvi and Qadir (1986).
10 Indeed, this appears to be the *belief* of most Muslim economists: as a result of the alleged Islamic reform all investors will get a higher return than they do at present. For instance, see Chapter 7 by Khan and Mirakhor (1987).
11 Thus, Chapra (1985) suggests that the Islamic financial reform should aim at substituting the present financial system by one that uses *only* equity-financing. It should be carefully noted that the present financial system, especially in the West, uses *both* these types of instruments – e.g., debentures and equities. Indeed, the debt-equity ratio is typically lower in the developed countries than in the developing countries. Thus, judged on the basis of this definition, the former will be more Islamic than the latter, which includes most of the Muslim countries!
12 Many empirical studies show that the changes in equity-financing are explained, among other factors, by the changes in the interest rate. See, for instance, Pindyck (1988), who, using the U.S. data, shows that the behaviour of the stock market is explained by such variables as real interest rates, the variance of stock returns, the rate of inflation, and the rate of profitability.
13 For example, see Siddiqi (1983).
14 The text only highlights the essence of a complicated proof as given in Naqvi and Qadir (1986).

11
TOWARDS A SOLUTION OF THE PROBLEM OF INTEREST

The preceding discussion gives a number of clues to solving the problem of replacing interest by an alternative procedure. First, we know that contrary to the widely held opinion, a 'universal' profit-and-loss-sharing (PLS) system – which performs various functions, as identified in Chapter 9, to keep the real sector of the economy growing along the steady-state path and regulates the concomitant financial operations – is *not* the answer to the economist's search for a viable policy alternative to the present financial system.[1] What we need instead is a *package* of financial policies, including the PLS-type instruments, to regulate the real and financial sectors of the economy.

Secondly, the liability exposure of different classes of savers and investors to risk must be limited, instead of the unlimited liability principle underlying the unrestricted PLS system.[2] This is only fair because, according to Islamic ethics, an individual cannot be made to shoulder a greater risk-burden than his financial position permits.[3]

Thirdly, the lending operations of the banks and other financial (investment and credit) institutions should be directed to transactions with a positive social value. If, on the other hand, the banks are forced to generate positive profits by investing in wasteful projects, then the entire process of generating profits will be contrary to the Islamic injunction. This is to restate the point, made earlier in Chapter 10, that the satisfaction of the ethical perception of Islam cannot be made contingent to the creation of profits regardless of the means.

REGULATING THE PLS SYSTEM

An important element of the solution, thus, is to operate the PLS system while keeping the limited-liability principle intact. Another element is that the monetary authority *guarantees* a minimum rate of return on the PLS deposits. A little reflection should show that none of these considerations should be anathema to the Islamic principles. Indeed, the two are inter-related because their objectives have the same common element: to protect the interests of the (poorer) lenders as opposed to those of the (richer) borrowers! But even from a purely technical point of view, the monetary authority can guarantee a (near) certain rate of return by indulging in some kind of open market operation on the PLS-scrips.[4] In this case, the actual rate of return is itself determined by the market, but the state intervenes when this rate falls below a certain acceptable limit.

Another way of satisfying the same conditions is to have most of the equity-financing done by commercial banks, particularly on behalf of those depositors who wish to earn more through investment in stocks.[5] These banks will then offer their depositors an investment portfolio, ranging from one hundred-percent safe deposits – the value of which will be guaranteed by the banks – to more 'risky' deposits, which promise varying degrees of returns to the depositors depending on the element of risk involved. The perfectly safe deposits will *at best* get a zero real return, even if these deposits are fully adjusted through a deposit-indexing scheme; but they may also get a negative real return if the cost-of-living adjustment is not one-hundred percent. On all the other deposits, there is a possibility of earning a positive *real* return, depending on the degree of risk the investors are willing to take. However, most of the profits attributable to uncertainty will accrue to commercial banks. Only a part of the profits will be passed on to the depositors, since their risk will be minimal.

In general, the banks and the financial institutions will have to devise portfolios containing alternative investment possibilities which are related to a *basic* real profit rate, which is zero. This basic rate will normally accrue to the marginal investor, who is a risk-averter. This marginal profit rate will be supported by the government at a level determined by the business conditions. All other profit rates on investments carrying varying degrees of risk will change as this basic rate changes. It may be noted that the nationalized banks can *normally* ensure a minimum positive profit on investment because they can easily offset the losses in one line of investment by the profits in other lines.

This scheme has the merit of imposing risk on the investors in proportion to their knowledge of the economic world. The small depositors should court no risk because they know little about the workings of the commodity-producing and financial sectors. By the same token, commercial banks will take the most risk because of their awareness of the intricate workings of modern industrial ventures, and because they know how to minimize their risk by 'spreading' it. Social justice demands some such apportionment of total risk – and of total profits – because there are some investors who are perfect risk-averters. It makes no sense to force them to take a risk even on their nest-egg savings. Obviously, they cannot do so and would rather stash away their savings in real estate, gold, jewellery, etc.

INDEXING OF THE RATES OF RETURN ON SAVINGS

Another proposal is to index the return on the PLS instruments to a suitable indicator of change in the economy's capacity to pay a specific rate of reward on savings. But it should be clear by now that an unrestricted, 'universal' PLS system may itself create severe problems of equity. Hence, to make it equitable, the PLS system must be restricted to those investors who can take risk; to those who, at any rate, invest in stocks instead of keeping their savings in deposits; and to the large borrowers.

We can now discuss a more comprehensive indexation scheme.

(a) The Principle of Indexation

The risk-averters can be identified as those who hold their savings in some kind of deposit instead of investing in ordinary stocks. The savings of this class are roughly equal to household savings. How does the government attract household savings in appropriate amounts? With the abolition of interest rates, some means must be found to increase household savings in the required amounts – by fixing the rate of return on permissible financial instrument at a high enough level to offset the saver's positive time preference.[6]

A perfectly legitimate and efficient way of achieving this objective is to index the rate of return on savings to a change in some appropriate reference variable – e.g., to changes in the price level, the nominal or real GDP, etc. If different classes of savers (investors) – those who save (invest) for a short term, medium term, or long term – are to be treated differently, as they should be, then the rate of indexation also will have to be related to the period for which the amount is saved (invested). This system should be legitimate even in the 'orthodox' sense because the rate of indexation will be related to the rate of change of the relevant (reference) variable, in which case the size of the return on savings is not predetermined.

Indexing Savings to Inflation: Deposits of all kinds can be indexed to changes in the price level. A 100-percent rate of indexation will simply keep the inflation-adjusted value of savings constant. To many classes of savers, a constant real value of savings should be enough incentive to save.

Indexing Savings to Inflation and the Rate of Growth of Real GDP: If the government must rely on encouraging household savings significantly, as is the case in Pakistan, then monetary policy should aim at a positive *real* rate of return on savings – that is, net of the inflation rate; at worst, a zero real rate of return should be guaranteed. Thus, the rate of indexation (to price level) will be equal to or *greater* than 100 percent. This principle will be applicable to special classes of deposits. Adjusting fully for inflation, the *maximum* increase in real terms may be set equal to the increase in *real* GDP, but that would not be correct. This is because, in general, the rate of return on capital is not equal to the growth rate of the GDP.[7] Also, it is only fair that capital(savings) be rewarded only in proportion to that part of the growth in the GDP (at factor cost) which can be imputed to it – equivalent to the combined contribution of interest, profit, and rent. To do that, the share of *wages* in the GDP must be subtracted from the total GDP.[8]

It may be interesting to note a few important characteristics of the proposed indexation scheme with reference to the Pakistani data. First, at the existing rate of increase in the price level and the GDP (in 1990–91), the maximum permissible nominal rate of return on household savings works out to be about 15.7

percent. This is significantly higher than the rates of return allowed at present on household savings. (The maximum rate now is around 12 percent.)[9] As household savings appear to have a positive relationship with changes in the nominal rate of return, this differential suggests that the indexation formula offers a significant improvement over the present system. Second, the size of the computed rate of return on the basis of indexation reflects an undesirable state of affairs in Pakistan with respect to the relative growth rates of the wage and non-wage components of the real GDP. The wage share in the GDP was 36.1 percent in 1986–87.[10] It was 35.0 percent in 1980–81, implying an increase in 7 years of only 1.1 percentage points. That this is an undesirable state of affairs can be seen by noting that in developed countries – in the U.S., for instance – the wage share of the GDP is about 70 percent. Now, if approximately a two-thirds wage share of the GDP is taken as a long-run objective for Pakistan, then to achieve it by the end of Year 2003, this share must rise by 4.1 percent over the next fifteen years. (At the present rate, it would take 56 years to achieve the stated objective!) The point to note is that this objective has to be pursued to satisfy the dictates of Equilibrium. This is because if the GDP and the price level grow at the postulated rate but the wage share does not increase, the rate of return on savings will not increase enough in the coming years.

(b) Reforming Lending Operations

The lending (borrowing) activities of the banks, however, cannot be indexed. This is because as inflation hurts the fixed-income group, it helps the variable-income group as the profits tend to increase in periods of inflation. How, then, can the lending operations be reformed according to the Islamic principles? Here a wide variety of policy instruments is available. The PLS system works well here because the borrowers (entrepreneurs) are risk-takers, and the big lenders (banks, investment companies, etc.) can also spread their risk. This system can be supplemented, as it is being done in Pakistan already, by a variety of policy instruments – the mark-up (or mark-down), *musharakah*, etc. But, in fact, the banks tend to concentrate on the mark-up, which mostly consists of government commodity operations. The result is that short-term lending is being encouraged even at the expense of long-term lending. Surely, this state of affairs must be rectified; but a balance between the short-and long-term borrowing will come only with the passage of time and more experience with the new (interest-free) policy instruments. Since all the policy instruments here are legitimate, the problem of further 'Islamizing' them is not involved.

Government and Inter-bank Transactions: A substantial part of the borrowing activities in Pakistan consists of government borrowing from the (nationalized) banking system to finance government deficit and inter-bank transactions, including those between the State Bank of Pakistan and the (nationalized) banks. All these transactions are virtually interest-based. Then, what can be done? One approach is to decree, as has been done in Iran, that such transactions (based on a fixed rate of return) are *not* interest. This is the simplest and most practical alternative.

The other approach is more complex. First, all efforts must be made to minimize deficit financing, which should be regulated by the legislature, even though this is easier said than done. Second, once the demand for government borrowing is substantially reduced, the interest charge on the remaining government borrowing may be converted into a service charge.

SUMMARY

The analysis presented in this and the preceding two chapters should make it clear that an unrestricted and universal PLS system will not be an adequate replacement of interest. Such a replacement will neither be efficient nor equitable. However, a properly restricted PLS system would be a useful policy. The main restrictions apply to minimizing the element of risk and guaranteeing a minimum rate of return on bank deposits. This principle is also applicable to the lending operations of the banks and small-scale enterprises. But, on the deposit side of the banking operations, a system of indexing deposits to an appropriate reference variable would be a useful policy.

NOTES

1 In a way, *nobody* thinks the PLS system to be the *only* alternative to interest. There is a vast array of permissible financial transactions. In Pakistan, we have, among others, the Participation Term Certificates,

mark-ups, hire-purchase, *Qard al-Hasana* (short-term interest-free loans), etc. See Iqbal and Mirakhor (1987) for an excellent discussion of the experiments with Islamic Banking in Pakistan and the Islamic Republic of Iran. One interesting result of the study is that, so far, the non-PLS policy instruments have *dominated* the PLS policy instruments in both the countries. In other words, the PLS system is *not* the dominant form of financing within the present Islamic financial system.

2 They may be lower-middle class savers because those who live on or near the 'poverty line' will not save anything. In most cases, they will have to depend on 'borrowing' (at zero rate) out of the Zakat funds, or on some other means.

3 The Quran makes clear the universal Islamic principle: 'No one should be charged beyond his capacity.' (2:233).

4 As discussed below, the minimum rate of return itself can be decided with reference to some variable, like the cost-of-living index, the GDP, etc.

5 This proposal also appears in Naqvi (1981), Appendix to Chapter 7.

6 The discussion in this section is based on Naqvi (1989).

7 Theoretically, the Golden Rule of Accumulation makes the rate of growth of the GDP to be a function of (per capita) capital alone. But this is not an operational principle, based as it is on highly restrictive assumptions.

8 Mathematically, such an indexation scheme can be formally expressed as

$$r = p + k.g$$

where r is the nominal rate of return on savings schemes, p is the inflation rate, k is the proportion of growth in the non-wage value-added in the total GDP growth, and g is the growth rate of the GDP in a specified period. For more on this, see Naqvi (1989).

9 The compound rates payable at maturity on the household savings schemes like Defence Saving Certificates, *Mahana Amdani* (Monthly Income) Account, Khas Deposit Certificates, and National Deposit Certificates during 1989–90 were, respectively, 15.6 percent, 14.9 percent, 13.4 percent, and 14.6 percent per annum.

10 Based on the preliminary estimates of National Income by Distributive Share prepared by the Federal Bureau of Statistics, Government of Pakistan.

Part IV
RAINBOW'S END

12

FROM THE IDEAL TO THE 'REALITY'

It may be useful now to look at the various logical, ethical, and economic issues raised in the preceding chapters from the viewpoint of their *implementability within the matrix of the present-day institutions*. Here we confront the problem of making a transition from the world of Islamic ideals to the reality of Muslim society.[1] It may be recalled that in Chapter 2 we invoked the concept of a Muslim society as a real-life counterpart of the (ideal) Islamic society. In the present chapter, we look at Muslim society to formulate singular (i.e., particular) statements based on actual experience so that the theories about the Islamic society, as developed in Chapters 3 to 10, can be falsified.[2]

THE CHALLENGE OF TRANSITION

Essentially, the problem of transition is to find the 'spaces' where compromises can be made without contradicting the central purpose of the Islamic ideals. The answer is not to reject such compromises as unIslamic, *because* they do not exactly conform to the ideal (textbook) situations. They should be seen as cases where the departures from the ideal *must* be made to make them implementable. Such real-life experimentation should then provide the basis for a new round of re-evaluation in terms of the Islamic law. True, such compromises may not decrease much the distance between a typical Muslim society and the Islamic society; but, notwithstanding the imperfections of the former, *such a society will still be recognizable as a distinct social entity inspired by the Islamic ideals*. And that is all that matters.

There were examples of such compromises even in the times of the Prophet. The most glaring case of compromise was the toleration of the institution of slavery. The Prophet did not abolish slavery straightaway presumably because the economic system was too dependent on this institution. Still, in keeping with the Islamic ideal, the equality of all men – including slaves – was unequivocally emphasized. Simultaneously, a series of steps were taken to 'humanize' the system – e.g., the freeing of slaves was seen as the highest form of piety as well as adequate atonement for other wrongs.[3] This was done presumably in the knowledge that, given Islam's emphasis on the equality of human beings, the institution will wither away with changes in the composition of the economy.

In our own times, one can easily find similar examples of compromises made by other economic systems. For instance, the socialistic ideals of the rule of the proletariat, and the equality of income and wealth, have either been diluted or replaced by other real-life institutions in the hope of a long-run realization of these ideals, or because such ideals are simply not achievable in their pristine forms. Similarly, the capitalistic ideals of the pure and perfect competition and unrestricted individual freedom have come to be replaced in practice by monopolistic competition – or by mere platitudes that more competition is better than less competition – and by situations where the individual's freedom is constrained to maximize social welfare. But, despite such compromises, these systems are still recognizable as a socialistic economy and a capitalistic economy, respectively.

This example highlights the point that *success in reforming real-life situations along Islamic lines lies in the ability to make strategic compromises within the framework of a series of reformist steps taken to reform the society on a wide enough scale.* This would entail a re-ordering of the priorities – or a sequencing of the reformist measures – so that some reforms are implemented while others are postponed until enough 'room' has been created for them. Needless to point out, making such creative compromises is not the same thing as a wilful subversion of the ideals. It is rather a methodical process of making suitable adjustments in the orthodox position with a view to implementing it within the ideological parameters.

FINANCIAL REFORMS IN PAKISTAN

We illustrate these abstract remarks by giving specific examples from Pakistan, where serious attempts have been made since 1979 to 'Islamize' the economy. The most outstanding such example is the financial reform undertaken in Pakistan to eliminate interest from the banking and the (non-banking) financial institutions.[4]

A series of innovative steps have been taken – e.g., the Participation Term Certificates (PTCs), lending on *Musharaka* (partnership), and the Mudarabah Certificates. Also, since 1985, commercial banks have been permitted to accept only Profit-and-Loss-Sharing (PLS) deposits. In addition, all development financial institutions (the DFIs) – e.g., the house building corporations, the National Investment Trust (NIT), etc. – have devised non-interest financial instruments consistent with the Islamic law.

In this section, we propose to test the hypothesis that a system run on the PLS principle will unambiguously raise the rate of return on savings, thereby ensuring a more just distribution of the total profits to savers. Since the thrust of the Islamic financial reform has been to Islamize the banking sector, we shall focus on it presently. The evidence is drawn from Pakistan, where the system has operated since 1983. Table 1 provides the details about the rate of return on the PLS and the non-PLS deposits of varying maturities. It makes clear the following points: (i) the rate of return on the PLS deposits has consistently *declined* since 1983, when the PLS system was introduced in full force;[5] (ii) the rate of return on the PLS deposits has fallen ever since the guarantees, designed to keep the returns on the PLS higher than on the non-PLS, were withdrawn in 1985. (Such guarantees were available during the 1979–85 period, when the commercial banks offered both the PLS and the non-PLS types of deposits); (iii) the rate of return on the PLS deposits, with a few exceptions, is *lower* than that on the non-PLS deposits. An important factor (not shown in the Table) explaining the lower rate of return on the PLS deposits is the shift in the savers' portfolio – the bank deposits declined while the investment in *interest-bearing financial instruments (e.g., Khas Deposits, Defence Saving Certificates, etc.) increased sharply.*[6] Yet another reason is the substantial increase in the number of *defaulting borrowers*

Table 1: Rates of Return on the PLS and the Non-PLS Deposits of Varying Maturities: 1983–1991

	Saving Deposits Non-PLS	Saving Deposits PLS	Six-months Deposits Non-PLS	Six-months Deposits PLS	One-year Deposits Non-PLS	One-year Deposits PLS	Two-year Deposits Non-PLS	Two-year Deposits PLS	Three-year Deposits Non-PLS	Three-year Deposits PLS	Four-year Deposits Non-PLS	Four-year Deposits PLS	Five Year & Above Deposits Non-PLS	Five Year & Above Deposits PLS
1983–84 June (Average)	7.62	–	9.92	–	10.51	–	10.93	–	11.81	–	12.46	–	12.45	–
1983–84 Dec. (Average)	7.62	7.85	9.87	10.02	10.50	11.0	10.80	11.6	11.73	12.40	12.33	12.94	13.43	13.43
1985–June Dec.	7.6 7.6	– 7.6	9.7 9.2	– 9.9	10.4 10.2	– 10.3	10.9 11.0	– 11.2	11.6 11.7	– 12.1	12.4 12.4	– 13.0	12.4 12.2	– 14.0
1986–June Dec.	7.6 7.0	– 7.1	9.0 9.2	– 9.2	9.4 8.0	– 9.7	10.5 11.0	– 10.5	11.4 11.6	– 11.5	11.9 12.3	– 12.2	12.0 12.3	– 13.0
1987–June Dec.	7.0 6.9	– 6.7	7.4 8.5	– 8.7	8.4 8.1	– 9.1	10.1 11.2	– 9.9	11.7 11.8	– 10.8	12.0 12.4	– 11.6	12.2 12.3	– 12.4
1988–June Dec.	7.3 6.9	– 6.7	8.2 7.8	– 8.5	8.1 7.7	– 8.8	10.6 10.0	– 9.6	11.3 10.7	– 10.4	10.5 10.0	– 11.3	12.1 11.5	– 12.0
1989–June Dec.	7.2 8.2	6.7 6.9	9.4 9.2	– 8.7	7.3 9.1	– 9.1	8.1 11.9	– 9.9	10.1 12.7	– 10.9	11.7 11.8	– 11.5	12.2 13.5	– 12.3
1990–June Dec.	7.4 10.1	7.1	10.6 11.6	8.9	8.4 11.3	9.4	8.9 14.7	10.1	8.2 15.7	10.9	12.6 14.6	11.5	11.5 16.8	12.3
1991–June	8.5		11.7		11.0		11.6		11.8		13.0		14.7	

Source: (i) *Pakistan Economic Survey, 1990–91*.
(ii) *Bulletin*, The State Bank of Pakistan, September 1989, May 1990, and December 1991.

Note: The Non-PLS deposits are those which are offered by the non-bank development financial institutions (DFIs).

ever since the interest option was withdrawan in 1985. This is in sharp contrast to the earlier practice of penalizing any such prolonging of the period of repayment by making the borrower pay the penalty interest rates as well. No such restriction is in force now. The result is that the evil effects of the borrower's irresponsible, even dishonest, behaviour are being suffered by the innocent depositors. This evidence directly contradicts the assertion that the PLS system will *always* ensure a fairer distribution of costs and benefits between the borrowers and the lenders.

It is interesting to note that with the introduction of the PLS system, the share of the time deposits in the total deposits has *declined*.

Table 2: Time Deposits in Pakistan since 1983

	Time Deposits	Growth Rate (%)
1983 June	49483	39.0
1984 June	59822	20.9
1985 June	64937	8.5
1986 June	76280	17.5
1987 June	80398	5.4
1988 June	84374	4.9
1989 June	77105	−8.6
1990 June	80241	4.1
1991 June	89233	11.2

Source: Bulletin, The State Bank of Pakistan, December 1991.

Thus, as shown in Table 2, with the exception of 1986 and 1991, the growth rate of the time deposits has declined since 1985 – and it was even negative in 1989! But, even more important, the growth rate of the time deposits has substantially declined as compared with 1983 – which shows that the 1985 withdrawal of the interest-option from the banking system has adversely affected its operational efficiency. This suggests that, because of the lower rate of return that it offers, the banking system has been incapacitated as a mobilizer of savings.[7]

A still more interesting observation is that in the process of implementing the Islamic financial reforms, the *form* of the policy instruments has changed. Contrary to the earlier intention, the package of policy instruments now contains fewer

PLS policy instruments and *more* non-PLS policy instruments. Indeed, within the first five years of its introduction, the *Mudarabah* and *Musharaka* types of lending all but disappeared from the bankers' portfolio; now nearly all lending transactions are being done on the mark-up basis. Furthermore, the introduction of the PLS system has been deferred with respect to the government and inter-bank transactions.[8] Indeed, all government borrowing from the public – and the borrowing from the banking system to finance the government deficit – as well as the inter-bank transactions, including those between the State Bank of Pakistan and the commercial banks, continue to be interest-based.[9]

How do we interpret this evidence? It should be obvious that it is not enough to *verify* the hypothesis noted above in a positive sense; but it is sufficient to *falsify* it. Almost every prediction of the theory – that with respect to the efficiency of the PLS as a mobilizer of savings by ensuring better rates of return to lenders, and that with regard to its equity – has been empirically contradicted. But this does not necessarily imply that the PLS is unworkable under all circumstances, and that we must abandon it in *toto*. As suggested in Chapter 11, a properly modified system can still work as a useful supplement to the other policy instruments.

THE PANGS OF TRANSITION

The criticism of the PLS system in the previous section highlights the need for a learning process to help make a transition to a legitimate and workable system.[10] But, in the process of experimentation with new modes of financing, efforts should be made to remove their shortcomings so that the lending operations of the banks become more efficient. Furthermore, with the provision of *advance* guarantees about a minimum rate of return, it should be possible to devise effective ways and means of operating the system. In other words, in order to work with the PLS system, its *form* may have to be changed. But to make such adjustments, it is essential that all kinds of evidence, both favourable and adverse, is continuously collected and critically analysed.

There is nothing sacrosanct about the specific financial arrangements adopted as part of the Islamization effort. Like all human institutions, such arrangements are also fallible and need to be improved upon continuously. It is a fact that the existing body of Islamic Law is mostly a collection of *interpretations* of the Divine Message by men of great learning who took cognizance of the socio-economic framework of their times. A dynamic reinterpretation of Islamic Law will have to be made to suit the needs of modern society.

Another fundamental problem relates to the scope of the Islamization process. We hold the view that it must be comprehensive – i.e., it should be undertaken *both* in the financial and the real sectors of the economy in an integrated fashion. The reforms in the real sector should focus on re-establishing the 'initial conditions' in accordance with the Islamic message and reorientating the production structure to meet the rising demand for wage goods. Furthermore, greater emphasis should be placed on universalizing education and providing a health-cover to 'the needy and deprived' within the framework of a wide-ranging social security system. In the financial sector, the emphasis should be on creating a *spectrum* of policy instruments to cater to the needs of both the risk-takers and the risk-averters. In this spectrum, the PLS-type instruments will figure, but with no claims to any priority on *Islamic* grounds, since no sanctity attaches to the institution of profit *per se*. If we do not clearly understand the *raison d'etre* behind the Islamic financial reforms – that they are about lowering the level of social exploitation and not just making the financial system more efficient – then the institutions run on the basis of profits alone can become as bad as the one using interest.

The 'Initial Conditions'

The first order of business to *initiate* a viable programme of Islamic reform is to focus on changing the 'initial conditions' – especially those relating to the basic structure of the society – in such a manner that the process of growth is associated with greater equality rather than with less equality.[11] This will come about when, freed from the barriers to social and economic mobility, every citizen is allowed access to the most extensive set of opportunities the society has to offer. Indeed, a stronger statement is possible: if in the initial situation the basic structure of the society is not such as will promote vertical and horizontal equity, then it will be even more difficult to achieve the objectives of an Islamic reform in subsequent situations because the initial inequities tend to snowball with the passage of time.[12]

Furthermore, it is impossible to achieve equality of *opportunity* without reducing the level of income inequality.[13] This point must be carefully noted by those who emphasize that the policy objective in an Islamic economy is an equalization of opportunities; and that the inequalities do not matter. *If not properly qualified, such a position is inconsistent.* This is because the capacity of the poor to participate in the economic process is determined decisively by their family's economic position.

Thus, a policy package relating to the 'initial conditions' must focus on: (i) reducing, though not eliminating, the inequalities in the distribution of wealth, including a reduction in the size of private property, particularly landed property; (ii) reorganizing industrial structure by relating the labour's share to the total profits of the industry; (iii) making a provision for an elaborate social security programme to help those living below the 'poverty line'; and (iv) taking decisive steps towards universal education. An effective and honest implementation of these policies should set out the preconditions of a socially just and dynamic Muslim society.

These matters have been discussed in the previous chapters. However, a few remarks on their relative importance in facilitating the process of transition should help clarify the basic theme of this chapter.

(i) Private Property: It should be quite clear that the institution of private property will have to be regulated as part of the Islamization programme. This is particularly true of those Muslim societies where the feudal systems occupy a position of importance. No economic harm will be done – indeed, great social benefits will flow – if steps are taken to abolish such economically counter-productive systems in which priority is accorded to the rights of non-cultivators over those of cultivators; and if all fallow and uncultivated lands are taken over by the state. In general, Islam recognizes private property rights; but such rights are directly related to the fact of cultivation which, as Taleghani (1982) notes, is the only basis of 'limited ownership'. All other lands and the natural resources like mines,

forests, public pastures, etc., belong to the state on the ground that these are the collective property of all people, and not of a few individuals; and that these will be normally managed by individuals on behalf of the state.[14] The recommendation for the confiscation of big land holdings after appropriate compensation gets support from the circumstantial evidence to the effect that these were mostly obtained as a reward for the anti-social services rendered by their recipients to colonial governments.[15]

When the confiscation of landed property by the state is not considered politically feasible, the income from such property should be heavily taxed. In particular, the imposition of capital-gains taxation on landed property should be fully justified – all the more so in a period of rapid inflation and steady urbanization, since both tend to escalate the capital values of real estate. Careful thought should also be given to the imposition of heavy death duties in order to liquidate private wealth within three generations after the death of its owner. Such taxes should be consistent with the *spirit* of the Islamic Law of Inheritance, which definitely rejects the individual's right to his private property after death. Furthermore, the individual's right to the earnings from his labour during his lifetime can at best be related to his own welfare and that of his children and grand-children, but it cannot be extended to justify the creation of dynastic oligarchies in the name of individual freedom.

(ii) Voluntary Combinations: To achieve distributive justice, it is desirable that, so far as possible, the productive activity in the society is carried out on a cooperative rather than a competitive basis. Hence, as part of the Islamization programme, the industrial sector will have to be reorganized along a two-tier system, which will allow the wage-earner a portion of the total profits as a bonus in addition to his fixed wage. This system is especially effective in increasing the productivity of the industries in the public sector by promoting participation of workers. Thus, besides promoting social harmony and industrial peace, such a system should also minimize the 'alienation' phenomenon noted by Marx in large industrial organizations. In this kind of participatory system, profits are distributed to the shareholders *minus* the financial provision for capital depreciation and other recurring costs plus a fixed contribution to the

national exchequer. The system should make an important contribution to democratize the industrialization process, with powerful built-in incentives for those who make an extraordinary contribution to production. It should also change the *power relations* in the industrial sector.

In sharp contrast, an economic system based *entirely* on free competition creates too many conflict situations without offering any mechanism for resolving such conflicts. It rewards much too liberally those who succeed, while it penalizes heavily the losers in the game.[16] The Islamic society will definitely strive to steer clear of such extremes by moderating both the reward for success and the penalty for failure. Such an attitude is strongly indicated because success and failure are not entirely attributable to merit, or to a lack of it, on the part of the economic agents. Chance factors intervene most of the time – as pure luck, too, sometimes – to decide the outcome of the relentless struggle for economic survival.

(iii) Universal Education: Providing universal education is an integral part of the Islamic economic reform. Indeed, income inequalities in the Islamic perspective can be justified only on the basis of the differences of knowledge among men. Modern studies on the economics of education make the point that education by itself does not reduce inequality, which is mostly due to the varying income levels from inherited private property. Indeed, as noted above, the equalization of the opportunities of education can be especially beneficial within the framework of an egalitarian reform package. To this end, it will be essential to initially provide for *unequal* opportunities by committing larger financial resources and physical facilities for the education of the poorer children. Nothing substantial in terms of either material growth or spiritual advancement can be gained on the basis of poor educational standards prevalent in most Muslim countries.[17] Hence, a sharp increase in the financial allocation for education will be required alongside a definite programme to reduce the existing inequalities of income and wealth.

SUMMARY

It is essential that a few lessons are learnt carefully to bring the Muslim societies nearer the Islamic ideals. First, *it will be wrong to think that the Islamic ideal, insofar as it is an ideal, can ever be achieved exactly.* The best we can do is to move in that direction, with the understanding that however hard we try, there will still be a large unfinished agenda on our hands. This is *not* to say that imperfections must be lauded *per se*; but only that once the direction of change is fixed in line with the Islamic ethical axioms, such efforts will also be justified. As in everything else in life, the best need not be the enemy of the good!

Second, during this process, many textbook versions of the Islamization programme which aim to achieve the ideals exactly will have to be modified with an eye to their implementability. What is not implementable in its pristine formulation, and only introduces an irresolvable conflict situation, must be either modified or discarded altogether *even if that is legitimate from an Islamic point of view.* In this context, careful thought should be given to the PLS principle, which in practice has failed so far to deliver the goods in the banking sector – even though this is where the Muslim economists thought their success was most certain.

Third, to fix the direction of Islamic reform, steps will have to be taken to focus on the initial conditions, so that economic growth is associated with the egalitarian goals of the Islamic economy. To that end, restructuring of the production, distribution, and consumption relations will be required. Steps taken to strengthen the effective demand of the poor by various redistributive measures must be accompanied by a programme to reorientate the production structure. Such a policy is more likely to produce, *within the allowability constraint*, the socially desirable consumption basket. In particular, not much can be achieved by way of Islamization unless the present capitalistic structure undergoes a profound transformation.

Fourth, the primary emphasis of a meaningful Islamization programme will have to be on reducing the absolute and relative levels of social and economic inequalities. Without this, no other social reform can produce the desired results. *To emphasize isolated policies – e.g., the abolition of riba – instead of pursuing a wide-ranging structural reform is bound to be a self-defeating exercise.* In particular, a viable programme of Islamic reform should include a rationalization of the structure of private property. We recognize Islamization as the *elan vital* of Muslim society, one that mobilizes favourable popular opinion and, thus, has a greater chance of success than one that leaves the appetite and imagination unexcited. But, to produce the best results, a reinterpretation of Islamic Law must be undertaken.[18]

NOTES

1 It may be noted that the transition in this chapter is not defined as the time needed to *fully* implement the Divine commandments. Doing so is an impossibility because accommodation of the timeless and institution-free message within the matrix of space and time must always be an incomplete process. In this sense, the transition period will be infinite.
2 Note that we do not say: '... to find singular statements from which theories about the Islamic society can be (inductively) derived.' Such a statement will require going from a *singular* (specific) statement to a *universal* statement – the familiar (impossible) Hume's problem of induction. See Popper (1980). See also ch. 2, n. 13 above.
3 Presumably, the system was not abolished because in those times the services sector, apart from a primitive agriculture, must have dominated the composition of the GNP. But, as noted in the text, the institution was humanized in keeping with the spirit of Islam. The Prophet set an example in his own household by exhorting his daughter, Fatima, to work on alternate days alongwith her slave. Zaid, a freed slave, was adopted by the Prophet as his own son and married to a relative of the Prophet. Indeed, in time, 'slaves among Muslims not only acquired equality of status but also became rulers, receiving the same recognition from the Ulama as the most exalted among the faithful' [Zakaria (1991)].
4 However, over the last decade or so, somewhat similar reforms have been attempted in several other Islamic countries as well. For a set of case studies evaluating such efforts, see Wilson (1990); Mangla and Uppal (1990). Also, Khan and Mirakhor (1990) make a rather specific comparison of Pakistan's experiences with Islamization with those of Iran.
5 In fact, this tendency has been observed by other researchers too. For instance, Gierths [in Wilson (1990)], while analysing the rates of return on 'savings accounts' in Pakistan for 1981–86, notes a sharp decline in them between 1985 and 1986. Of course, as noted in the text, we know that this trend has actually continued beyond 1986.
6 The Iranian experience with interest-free banking has been broadly similar with respect to its effects on the rates of return on bank deposits. To make matters much worse, a high rate of inflation has

led to strongly negative *real* rates of return, having adverse effects on the household savings.
7 For relevant information see the relevant issues of *Pakistan Economic Survey*, an annual publication of the Government of Pakistan.
8 In fact, since the Government of Pakistan borrows directly from the public at a rate higher than that paid on the PLS deposits of the banks, this may have been one of the factors that has hurt efforts at increasing 'intermediation' – one of the avowed goals of Islamization of banking in Pakistan [Khan and Mirakhor (1990), p. 373].
9 As noted in the previous chapter, the theologians in the Islamic Republic of Iran have decreed that such transactions are *not* interest. [Iqbal and Mirakhor (1987) p. 24.] Coming from a fundamentalist government insistent on transforming the entire economy along Islamic lines, this illustrates a case where reality dictates a reinterpretation of the Islamic Law.

It may be noted, however, that in practice while the inter-bank lending in Iran is carried out at a (fixed) positive 'rate of return', the government borrows from the banking system without paying any such return. [Khan and Mirakhor (1990), p. 373].
10 As an example of the possible difficulties that may be encountered during the transitory period, it may be noted that Iran had to hurriedly put 20,000 persons through a course in Islamic Banking just to initiate the process of Islamization of the financial sector. [Aryan in Wilson (1990), p. 156].
11 Inter-class and intra-class equalization of the economic conditions is essential not only to ensure distributive justice but also to guarantee human freedom. This has been observed by many an acute social philosopher. For instance, Tocqueville (1944) pointedly remarked that liberty is inconsistent with gross inequalities of 'social conditions'. Furthermore, Lindahl (1960) emphasized the importance of a 'just distribution of property to begin with', to lay the preconditions of securing equity. The most influential recent contribution emphasizing the importance of an 'initial just order' is that by Rawls (1971).
12 In dynamical, mathematical systems, once a set of starting values leading to acceptable terminal values has been specified, it is possible to determine an entire time path of the variables that satisfy the necessary conditions for optimality. The dynamics of the social system is broadly similar in character, even though the outcome of specific policies cannot be as infallibly predicted as in mathematics.
13 For a detailed demonstration of this thesis, see Naqvi and Qadir (1985); and also Jencks *et al.* (1972). Another influential voice is that of Thurow (1969).
14 Sadr (1982) also holds a similar point of view.
15 The present-day practice of granting fertile lands as a reward for rendering the so-called meritorious services must also be discontinued, particularly because scarce fertile land gets allocated to those who are the least fit to make an effective use of it, not the least

reason is that such grants are also not in accordance with the spirit of the Islamic law. Indeed, in the early Islamic period, the free gift of land was limited only to 'dead' lands, which could then be reclaimed by the owners at their cost. It was only during the Umayyad period that the doling out of top-quality lands started, mostly to the members of the royal family, as a system of disguised bribery.

16 As is well known, free competition helps the society only to attain a point on the 'efficiency locus', thereby satisfying a marginal welfare condition. However, each point on the efficiency locus is consistent with a distribution of income that diverges sharply from the social optimum. Hence, it is necessary to specify a 'first-best' distribution of income to attain 'social bliss' – a state which will be defined differently in each society *in keeping with its ethical norms*. Furthermore, the maximum welfare thus achieved will not be unique, without specifying the distribution of income, which is determined not by marginal conditions but by the ethical norms of the society. See Naqvi (1981).

17 In this connection, it is interesting to recall the historic U.S. Supreme Court ruling which maintained that school segregation led to unequal performance even when the schools were of an equal standard. Hunt's (1961) seminal contribution confirmed the thesis that educability is directly related to socio-economic status and intelligence. Schultz's (1960) pioneering work which analyses the economic effects of education, points in the same direction.

18 Such a process has the best chance of success in a democratic set-up, i.e., if it is carried out in the national parliaments. Gradually, steps will have to be taken by a parliament of all Islamic countries to resolve the difficult issues in the interpretation of the Divine Law.

13
TOWARDS A NEW SOCIAL REALITY

An attempt has been made in this book to delineate, albeit with a broad brush, the distinguishing features of Islamic economics as a discipline in its own right; and to emphasize that it is a discipline which displays its normative character strongly enough to set it apart from all other kinds of economics, including the mainstream neoclassical economics. We have used the axiomatic approach to show what it means to unify the ethical and economic perceptions of Islam into a single comprehensive analytical framework. To this end, the Islamic ethical principles have been systematized into a set of ethical axioms in order to derive all the key (refutable) hypotheses about the rules of economic behaviour in the Islamic economy. This logically consistent procedure – now widely practised in mainstream economics – should allow us to test these hypotheses about the *Islamic* society against the experience of a modern *Muslim* society – the latter serving as the real-life analytical counterpart of the former.

It needs to be understood that the axiomatic approach is the *only* procedure to derive – from the aforementioned ethical axioms – logically valid statements about an Islamic economy, and to establish the Islamic (or un-Islamic) character of any economic statements. Any other way of going about the task will be indecisive. For instance, any attempt to reconstruct Islamic economics, brick by brick, *on the basis* of isolated observations of the real (Muslim) world – i.e., through the so-called inductive method – is doomed on strictly logical grounds.[1] By the same token, one cannot insist, in an ultra-traditionalist vein, that to establish the Islamic credentials of each and every (valid) economic statement we must find a *sanad* (authority) in the form of an explicit opinion of some casuist. This, for the simple reason that it is not possible to identify a corresponding statement in the *fiqh* (Islamic juridical) literature. As it is, the axioms in any religion, including Islam, are God-given and eternal while theology is man-made and subject to reinterpretation from time to time.

The next step is to set up procedures to test, even if only heuristically, the validity of the basic postulates of Islamic economics. For if there was no hope ever to test – or, to use Popper's terminology, to *falsify* – the key economic statements about Islamic economics, then our discipline would be still-born. For instance, if the basic assertions of Islamic economics about its essential normative character were also not a potentially 'observable' phenomenon – besides being a philosophical proposition – in a typical Muslim society, then its hard-core generalizations would be no more than a collection of *irrefutable* moral platitudes.

However, as noted in the preceding pages, there is no reason for us not to meet the demands of scientific validity. The real-life behaviour of a 'representative' Muslim displays the distinctive trait of combining ethics with his economic activities on account of his *belief* in the Divine Presence. From this point of view, it is of no consequence whatsoever that present-day Muslim societies do not always faithfully reflect the Islamic ideals – for *which* societies conform exactly to their ideals? The relevant point is that Muslim societies, despite some of their deviant practices, are clearly recognizable as a community of Muslims. Even as a pale shadow of the ideals that he believes in, a representative Muslim's behaviour is sufficiently different from persons belonging to other religious cultures so as to warrant a separate scientific treatment.

A LEITMOTIF

The essential contextual relativity of this formulation of Islamic economics bespeaks not only the relativity of economic science but also those parts of the Islamic law which relate to economic matters.[2] As the process of Islamic reform gathers momentum in modern Muslim societies, it will become essential to reformulate some of the orthodox (theoretical) views on economic matters. In many Muslim countries – especially in Pakistan and Iran –

the time has come to do just that; so that in the next cycle of intellectual development *a priori* reasoning on Islamic economics can hopefully be confronted with empirical evidence.

It is out of this interaction of the ideals and the reality that a new vision will be born of a dynamic Muslim society. But this (continuous) process of reaching out to the Islamic ideals is not so much a sign of imperfection as of intellectual vitality and dynamism. In the process of idea formation, there is no such thing as the final word or a definitive answer. The crucial point of our analysis has been that, instead of an *ad hoc* approach, the Islamic ethical axioms should be made the basis of logically valid and empirically testable economic statements about an Islamic economy. Indeed, without such axioms, it will not be possible to establish the objective validity of the value judgements made in Islamic economics. This is what we have sought to accomplish in this book.

The *deductive* method used in the present study to derive the basic economic statements relevant to the Islamic economy has the merit of recognizing the following characteristics of the Islamic vision of economic processes:

(i) Islam insists that its ethical philosophy *dominate* the economic universe.
(ii) Islam further stipulates that not just ethics but an ethics based on religion must be accepted as the source of the basic postulates needed to make valid economic generalizations.
(iii) The practices of Muslim societies do reflect, however imperfectly, the dominance of Islamic ethical beliefs. The unquestioning acceptance of the Divine Presence as a *fact of life* moulds the economic behaviour of the representative Muslim – and not only of a devout Muslim – in a significant manner.

To comprehend this ethical dimension, we use four axioms, namely, Unity, Equilibrium, Free Will, and Responsibility. The logical link between these axioms and the basic rules of economic behaviour in an Islamic economy has been made explicit by a number of auxiliary hypotheses. With the help of this analytical method, we show in this book that an Islamic economic system, on the logical plane, *exists* apart from all existing economic systems like socialism, capitalism, and the welfare state. But this is not all. The basic hypotheses of Islamic economics are also *falsifiable* within the matrix of real-life Muslim societies – in the sense that at least some of them are capable of being formulated into refutable hypotheses.

In relation to the world of ideals, Muslim society is admittedly imperfect but this is not a disadvantage from a scientific point of view. Indeed, this is an 'advantage', if only because a perfect society is beyond justice and does not need any explanations. It is the same with all economic systems. For instance, despite many compromises, capitalism is distinguished by its insistence on man's absolute right to own private property; and by a perception that accepts the primacy of the general principles of competition motivated by self-interest. Socialism, by contrast, insists on collective welfare, and relies on the visible hand of the state to maximize social welfare. Correspondingly, its attitude towards private property is nihilistic. But, in practice, the capitalistic and socialistic societies, too, are nothing but pale shadows of the textbook versions of capitalism and socialism. It is no different for real-life Muslim economy.

THE MAINSPRINGS OF ISLAMIC ECONOMIC PHILOSOPHY

An important general point, which is the central theme of this book, is that ethics is implicit in all social systems and not only in the Islamic system. True, both capitalistic and socialistic economists protest to the contrary – the former insisting on its objective rather than normative character, the latter emphasizing its 'scientific' nature. But one does not have to go too far to discover that a lot of what is presented as amoral, scientific objectivity is nothing more than a thinly disguised championing of a set of value judgements – e.g., the Pareto-optimality principle used in neoclassical economics is in fact a vote for the *status quo*, even if it be unjust, as long as the efficiency criterion is satisfied. Hence, our insistence to make explicit and visible the ethical nature of Islamic economics is perfectly legitimate from a scientific point of view.

The evidence presented thus far confirms that Islam seeks to create a new balance between individual freedom and social responsibility – a balance based on a regime of voluntarism and informed by a deep sense of the Divine Presence. Thus, the practical shape given to the ethical constraints of Islam represents no more than a minimum element of coercion. For instance, by equating voluntary giving to the poor and the needy – those who have a *right* in the wealth of the rich – to spiritual salvation, the individual has been asked to tread 'the middle way' in order to be seen as acting rationally. This is Islam's distinction, one that separates it from all other 'isms'. It is, thus, legitimate to state that Islam's economic perception differs from the perception of all other economic systems by this *explicit* inclusion of consequentialist value judgements – i.e., those which evaluate the state of affairs by reference to the welfare of the least-privileged in society.

However, the statement that the Islamic economic system is a recognizable entity does *not* mean that it sits apart from its (non-Islamic) environment. Indeed, Islam would not subscribe to the Spenglerian view, according to which social systems grow up in hot-house conditions with little inter-systemic borrowing. On the other hand, Islam displays a healthy attitude of recognizing and assimilating that which is congenial to its genius, while rejecting that which is incompatible with its native character. Being the last revealed religion, Islam has displayed its power to synthesize the extant knowledge, to transmute it into its own mould creatively, and to improve upon it before finally accepting it.[3] In particular, the Islamic economic system will have to learn from the successes (and failures) of capitalism, socialism, and the welfare state. An uncompromising rejectionist attitude towards all existing economic systems is nothing more than intellectual nihilism – and, therefore, counterproductive in the extreme.

Notwithstanding its distinct normative character, an essential component of the Islamic perspective is the explicit recognition of man's 'possessive' and materialistic instincts: 'And lo! in the love of wealth he is violent' (100:8). But while recognizing this, Islam does not *glorify* un-altruistic behaviour, nor does it treat it as the point of departure for economic generalizations. Instead, it de-emphasizes such instinct in favour of voluntaristic altruism: 'Wealth and children are an ornament of life of the world. But the good deeds which endure are better in thy Lord's sight for reward, and better in respect of hope' (18:47). In the same vein, although man is seen as a free agent endowed with

Free Will, the freedom to make all sorts of choices is balanced by a deep sense of responsibility so as to maximize social welfare.

THE CONSEQUENCE-SENSITIVITY OF THE ISLAMIC ECONOMIC PHILOSOPHY

Unlike the Pythagorean scale of values, according to which a distinction is made between the life of contemplation and the life of action, Islam seeks to synthesize these two aspects of man's life into a unitary perspective in which the distinction between the secular and the spiritual becomes blurred if not totally irrelevant. It is this synthesis which forms the basis of the consequence-sensitive Islamic economic philosophy. Faced with a state of *zulm* (Disequilibrium), man must act to the best of his ability to restore *adl-wal-ihsan* (Equilibrium). Instead of acting the cowardly ostrich, man must try his best to roll back the tide of injustice to preserve the beauty of life, which God has created in His own image. This concept of freedom, if implemented, would help release man from the chains of an irrelevant past, from the slavery of other men, and from supine submission to one's own greed.

In this consequence-sensitive scenario, Islam lays the maximum emphasis on properly using man's innate *discretionary* faculties. Life does not come to a Muslim as a ready-made recipe that can be applied to all situations; instead, it presents itself to him as a deep mystical reality, whose mysteries can only be grasped slowly by the inquiring mind: 'We shall show them Our portents on the horizons and within themselves until it will be manifest unto them that it is the Truth' (41:53). It is only by exercising to the full his God-like faculty of reason that man can realize his viceregal *virtuality*; but to do that, reason must be buttressed by knowledge; faith fortified by habits of contemplation.

Equipped with both reason and faith, man must seek a social order based on Equilibrium established through a *conscious process*. It is thus that Islam enjoins the rectification of excessive concentration of income and wealth – especially that which flows from feudalist social structures.[4] Similarly, the concentration of political power in the hands of a few individuals (i.e., oligarchy), or in the state (i.e., dictatorship), is contrary to the

Islamic ideal for the simple reason that it destroys human freedom.

In moving towards the Islamic ideal and inducing people to live a life according to its dictates, the state will have to play a corrective role, *without claiming any fundamental rights of its own*. There is nothing Orwellian about this conception precisely because state intervention in the Islamic society is limited to implementing a socio-economic programme based on the dictates of Islamic ethics. A state that limits itself in this way would be qualitatively different from an oppressive totalitarian regime which arrogates to itself the natural right to decide between right and wrong. Since Islamic ethics clearly includes guaranteeing of human freedom, an Islamic state can never impose tyranny on the Muslims; *if it does, it is the collective responsibility of the Muslims to rebel against such tyranny*. True, Islam emphasizes the maintenance of social harmony; but only if the texture of such harmony has been woven by *adl* and *ihsan*, and not if it is made of *zulm*. This right of a Muslim to rebel against tyranny, even if it is imposed by another Muslim, is one of the most jealously guarded Islamic principles, and has been practised by Muslims in different times at different places.[5]

WHY AN ISLAMIC ECONOMY?

The question may be asked at this point: is it not possible to achieve the objectives of an Islamic economy within the parameters of the existing economic systems? After all, this would appear to be a 'safer' strategy to achieve the basic Islamic egalitarian objectives – e.g., individual freedom, distributive justice, economic growth, employment generation, and universal education. Why, then, opt for a largely untried Islamic economic system, taking a plunge into the unknown? There are at least two main reasons why an Islamic economic system is needed to resolve the various social and economic problems that the Muslim countries face at present.

Firstly, if it is accepted, consciously or unconsciously, that economic behaviour is ultimately conditioned by religious beliefs, then it should not be too difficult to understand that the coexistence of incompatible religious beliefs and modes of economic behaviour is bound to end up in intellectual and moral confusion. This is especially the case since Islam insists on ethical values; and because a representative Muslim's belief in the Divine Presence conditions his economic behaviour profoundly. In such ethical environment, any separation of economics from ethics *and* religion will be both artificial and counter-productive.

Secondly, even though in broad outlines the Islamic prescription is similar to what may be offered by any egalitarian economic system, the reasons for doing so are not the same. As pointed out earlier, the Islamic approach to economic development aims to promote material growth within the wider ethical context. To satisfy the dictates of Unity, economic growth must not be inimical to spiritual advancement. Such a 'composition' is automatically guaranteed because, in the Islamic perspective, the *ethically constrained* economic actions of man also point the way to his spiritual salvation. For instance, as noted above, the act of giving (e.g., *zakat*) is not only a redistributive device to alleviate social misery; it is also a means to achieve spiritual ascent. The net effect of this fusion of the material and ethical aspects in the framework of Islamic thought is to introduce a powerful element of 'voluntarism' into man's economic behaviour, since the reasons for growing economically are both material and spiritual. Needless to add, the two forces acting together must be more powerful than just the one – even for attaining strictly materialistic objectives.

THE FORCE OF ISLAMIC MORALITY

To be *seen* on the side of 'right', the Muslims must be committed to a societal framework in which human freedom is guaranteed and selfishness is not accepted as a virtue. Reminding themselves of this basic characteristic of the Islamic society, its members must 'expand' their inner selves to reach out to higher social ideals. But to do that, a mechanical and irrational reaction behaviour – of going from one extreme to another – must be replaced by a conscious effort to stick to the 'middle course'. Muslims will have to anchor their thought processes to the idea of a social balance and harmony, reflecting Islam's idealistic commitment to Equilibrium. Furthermore, in the Islamic system, man will be aware of his theomorphic potentialities to save himself from the lengthening shadows of 'alienation'. However, to bring about such profound attitudinal changes in a real-life

Muslim society, it will take nothing less than a moral revolution both at the individual and the social levels.

At the individual level, such a moral revolution will come about by deepening the sense of responsibility towards own self and fellow men to appreciate that true freedom flows from breaking down the demoralizing chains of avarice and selfishness. At the social level, such laws and institutions will have to be created as safeguard various kinds of freedoms – including the freedom from want and poverty. It is a challenge of the first order for Muslim economists to model these moral attitudes and learn more about their scientific properties. Their mettle will be tested by their willingness to go through the challenge-response ordeal, by their persistence with it, and by their ability to come up with *non-trivial* answers that are both legitimate and acceptable to the modern mind. To a Muslim wedded to Islam's consequence-sensitive moral philosophy, a policy of inaction towards social institutions should be totally unacceptable. The ethical principle of Responsibility regards a meek acceptance of social injustice as a grave dereliction. Although discharging this responsibility is not easy, yet it must be done to create a meaningful future.[6] The success of such a momentous mission will require the creation of an environment where human freedom flowers and finds new avenues of creative fulfilment.

THE ROAD TO SUCCESS

To crown the Islamization process with success, it is essential to realize the basic objectives. A series of steps need to be taken to change the *status quo* in Muslim societies. A beginning can be made, for example, by casting out the feudalistic social structures which have dehumanized Muslim societies and so far compromised both their economic and moral possibilities. Only then will a 'fluid' social structure be born – one that will be free of oppressive rigidities. *The superiority of the Islamic solution to the capitalistic and socialistic solutions will be ultimately established not by reference to its alleged Divine origin but by its success in ensuring social justice with human dignity.* Thus, among its basic policy objectives must figure the removal of serious problems such as poverty, illiteracy, and avoidable diseases. And this should be done not to patronize the poor, but because the poor have a moral and legal *right* in the wealth of the rich – a right which, according to the Quran, must be restored to them. Such a programme may appear to those who are in the habit of putting every new idea into some carefully labelled box an extreme 'leftist' philosophy; but Islam would unequivocally reject such a label; it, instead, calls its programme the 'straight path' – of social harmony.

Reassertion of Islamic values in a world of material affluence offers both an opportunity and a challenge to the Muslims. It is an opportunity: because modern societies – raised largely on the capitalistic principles – seem to have traded moral excellence for material prosperity. Islam can lead the way by showing that both can (and must) be achieved together. But this can be done only by shedding the hypocritical glorification of the cult of poverty, which some tyrannical (Muslim) regimes have used to their advantage. Indeed, *equal access to material plenitude, which is secured without sacrificing moral rectitude, is a fundamental right of every Muslim*. It is also a challenge: because if we fail to respond to it constructively, we will be relegated to the back-waters of history. A societal reordering, carried out on the basis of Islam's ethical precepts, will be an exclusively Islamic gift to the Muslims – indeed, to all well-meaning humanity. Instead of enduring an enervating schizophrenia, born of an inner split between the calls of the flesh and the beckoning of the soul, Islam offers a message of hope to mankind; it calls for exercising freedom while contributing to social harmony and world peace. Once this is fully realized, the entire world – and not Muslims alone – will have an interest in the success of the Islamic experiment.

The social ideals of Islam should convince the Muslims as well as the non-Muslims that true freedom comes of an abandonment of the desire for transient things, no less than by going forward with a passionate will for that which is permanent: 'Naught is the life of the world save pastime and a sport. Better far is the abode of the Hereafter for those who keep their duty (to Allah)' (6:32). However, this is not offered as a prescription to evade reality. The seeker after Truth, not resiling from the chilling blast of the bitter realities of life, will have to endure a long march through the night to catch the first rays of the rising sun. It is only by transmuting the desire for justice into the crucible of right ideas and purposeful actions that the present-day exploitative social systems can be changed. Those who live in the vision of the 'right', as Islam's ethical philosophy of the right signifies, must descend into the real world to turn the oppressive 'facts' of life into just forms – forms that will last – with the assurance of a manifold reward in the Hereafter: 'Whatsoever good ye send before you for your souls, ye will surely find it with Allah, better and greater in the recompense' (73:20).

NOTES

1 See Popper (1980); and also Chapter 2 of the present book for a full explanation of the remarks in the text.
2 Iqbal's (1986) observation in this regard is worth noting: 'The only course open to us is to approach modern knowledge with a respectful but independent attitude and to appreciate the teachings of Islam in the light of that knowledge, even though we may be led to differ from those who have gone before us' (p. 78).
3 As Nasr (1979) points out, 'this peculiarity of Islam as the last religion in the prophetic cycle gives it the power of synthesis so characteristic of this tradition' (p. 36).
4 It is interesting to note that Islam emphasized an equitable distribution of wealth several centuries before the socialists demanded it. The philosophy of pious Muslims like Abu Dharr (d. 652), reflecting the *practice* of the Prophet's family and many of his Companions, suggested bringing about an *absolute* equality in income distribution.
5 The first demonstration of this principle came not long after the death of the Prophet when his grandson (Husayn) fought the decisive battle of Karbala (in Iraq) against Yazid, a *Muslim* tyrant.
6 It may be interesting to note that Toynbee (1963) characterizes an 'active response' to the forces of social disintegration as 'an awakening to a sense of Unity which broadens and deepens as the vision expands from the Unity of mankind, through the Unity of the cosmos, to embrace the Unity of God'. In the Islamic perspective, the chain of causation is exactly the reverse of what Toynbee prescribes: it proceeds from the *belief* in the Unity of God, to the Unity of the cosmos, and then finally to the Unity of mankind.

REFERENCES

'Abduh, Shaykh Mohammad (1908). *Risala al-Tawhid*. First published in 1897, 2nd edn revised by Rashid Rida, 1908; 18th edn., 1957. Translated by Ishaq Musa'ad and Kenneth Cragg (1966) as *The Theology of Unity*. London: Allen & Unwin (Translation of the 18th edn., 1957).

Ahmad, Khurshid (ed.) (1976). *Islam: Its Meaning and Message*. London: Islamic Council of Europe.

────── (1981). 'Foreword' to Syed Nawab Haider Naqvi. *Ethics and Economics: An Islamic Synthesis*. Leicester: The Islamic Foundation.

al-Arabi, Ibn (1957). *Ahkam al-Quran* (Text in Arabic). Cairo. pp. 243–244.

Aleshina, I. V. (1976). *Problems of Modelling in the Developing Countries* (English translation). Leningrad.

Ali, Abdullah Yusuf (1938). *The Holy Quran: Text, Translation, and Commentary*. Lahore: Sheikh Muhammad Ashraf.

Ali, Ahmed (1984). *Al-Qur'an: A Contemporary Translation*. Karachi: Akrash Publishing.

Ali, Syed Ameer (1922). *The Spirit of Islam*. London: Christophers.

Anwar, Muhammed (1987). *Modelling Interest – Free Economy, a Study in Macro-economics and Development*. Herndon, Va.: International Institute of Islamic Thought.

Aron, Raymond (1968). *Main Currents in Sociological Thought-I*. New York: Doubleday.

────── (1970). *Main Currents in Sociological Thought-II*. New York: Doubleday.

Arrow, Kenneth J. (1951). *Social Choice and Individual Values*. Cowles Foundation, Monograph 12. New York: John Wiley & Sons, Inc.

────── (1979). 'The Property Rights Doctrine and Demand Revelation under Incomplete Information'. Chapter 2 in Michael J. Boskin (ed.), *Economics and Human Welfare: Essays in Honour of Tibor Scitovsky*. New York: Academic Press.

────── (1985). 'Economic history: A necessary though not Sufficient Condition For an Economist.' *American Economic Reivew*, Papers and Proceedings 75(2). May. 320–23.

REFERENCES

Asaria, Mohammad Iqbal (1982). 'Book Review'. *Crescent* (Ontario, Canada) August 16–31.
Al-Ash'ari, Abu'l Hasan (1929). *Maqalat al-Islamiyyin*, ed. Helmut Ritter. Istanbul.
Atkinson, A. B. (1989). Poverty. In John Eatwell, Murray Milgate, and Peter Newman. (eds.) *Social Economics (The New Palgrave)*. London: Macmillan.
Bell, Richard (1953). *Introduction to the Quran*. Edinburgh.
Blaug, Mark (1985). *Economic Theory in Retrospect*. Cambridge: Cambridge University Press.
Bliss, Christopher (1990). 'Equal Rates of Profit.' In John Eatwell, Murray Milgate and Peter Newman. (eds.) *Capital Theory (The New Palgrave)*. London: Macmillan.
Boer, De (1970). *The History of Philosophy in Islam*. London: Luzac & Company Ltd.
Boisard, Marcel A. (1987). *Humanism in Islam* (English translation). Indianapolis: American Trust Publications. (Originally published in French in 1979).
Briggs, A. (1961). The Welfare State in Historical Perspective. *Archives Europeenes de Sociologie*. 2(2). pp. 221–59.
Caterphores, George (1990). Alienation. In John Eatwell, Murray Milgate, and Peter Newman (eds.) *Marxian Economics (The New Palgrave)*. London: Macmillan.
Chapra, M. Umer (1981). 'Book Review'. *The Muslim World Book Review*. Vol. 2, No. 1, pp. 21–26.
—— (1985). *Towards a Just Monetary System*. Leicester: The Islamic Foundation.
Coleman, James S. (1989). Equality. In John Eatwell, Murray Milgate, and Peter Newman. *Social Economics (The New Palgrave)*. London: Macmillan.
Deane, Phyllis (1983). 'The Scope and Method of Economic Science'. *Economic Journal*. Vol. 93, No. 369, pp. 1–12.
Debreu, Gerard (1959). *Theory of Value*. Cowles Foundation, Monograph 17. New York: John Wiley & Sons, Inc.
Diamond, P. and J. A. Mirrlees (1971). Optimal Taxation and Public Production: I: Production Efficiency *American Economic Review*, January 8–27; and II: Tax Rules. *American Economic Review* 61, June, 261–8.
Eaton, Charles le Ga (1987). 'Man'. Chapter 19 in S. H. Nasr (ed.), *Islamic Spirituality*. London: Routledge and Kegan Paul.
Friedman, Milton (1953). *Essays in Positive Economics*. Chicago: University of Chicago Press.
Gemignani, M. C. (1968). *Basic Concepts of Mathematics and Logic*. London: Addison-Wesley Publishing Co.
Gibb, H. A. R. (1968). *Islam*. London: Oxford University Press.
Gibb, H. A. R. and J. H. Kramers (1961). *The Shorter Encyclopaedia of Islam*. Ithaca, NY: Cornell University Press.
Gough, I. (1979). *The Political Economy of Welfare State*. London: Macmillan.
Gough, I. (1989). Welfare State. In John Eatwell, Murray Milgate, and

Peter Newman (eds.), *Social Economics (The New Palgrave).* London: Macmillan.
Guillaume, Alfred (1954) *Islam.* Harmondsworth: Penguin.
Hadley, G. (1964). *Linear Algebra.* London: Addison-Wesley Publishing Co.
Hahn, F. H., and Martin Hollis (1979). *Philosophy and Economic Theory.* London: Oxford University Press.
Haque, Ziaul (1977). *Landlord and Peasant in Early Islam.* Islamabad: Islamic Research Institute.
—— (1981). 'Book Review'. *The Muslim* (Daily), (Islamabad), 1st May.
—— (1985). *Islam and Feudalism: The Economics of Riba, Interest and Profit.* Lahore: Vanguard Books Ltd. (Chapters 3 and 4 especially).
Harrison, Ross (1989). Jeremy Bentham. In John Eatwell, Murray Milgate, and Peter Newman (eds.), *The Invisible Hand (The New Palgrave).* London: Macmillan.
Harsanyi, John C. (1991). Value judgements. In John Eastwell, Murray Milgate and Peter Newman (eds.), *The World of Economics (The New Palgrave).* London: Macmillan.
Hashmi, Alamgir (1986). *The Worlds of Muslim Imagination.* Islamabad: Gulmohar Press.
Hausman, Daniel M. (1984). *The Philosophy of Economics: An Anthology.* Cambridge: Cambridge University Press.
Hazm, Ibn. (1350 A.H.) *Al-Muhalla* (Text in Arabic). Vol. 8. Cairo: Idara al Muniriyya.
Hume, David (1748). *An Enquiry Concerning Human Understanding.* (Reprinted in 1955). Indianapolis: Bobbs-Merrill.
Hunt, J. M. (1961). *Intelligence and Experience.* New York: Ronald Press.
Iqbal, Mohammad (1986). *The Reconstruction of Religious Thought in Islam.* ed. M. Saeed Sheikh. Lahore: Institute of Islamic Culture. First published in 1934.
Iqbal, Zubair, and A. Mirakhor (1987). *Islamic Banking.* Washington, D.C.: The International Monetary Fund.
Ingersoll, J. E. (1989). Interest Rates. In John Eatwell, Murray Milgate, and Peter Newman (eds.), *Finance (The New Palgrave).* London: Macmillan.
Jafri, Syed Husain M. (1988). A Historical Review of the Development of Islamic Thought. In Jafri (Ed) *Iqbal, the Reconstruction of Islamic Thought.* (Text in Urdu). Karachi: Pakistan Area Study Centre.
Jauhri, Talib (1984). *Islamic Economics* (Urdu). Karachi: Mass Printers.
Jencks, Christopher, *et al.* (1972). *Inequality.* New York: Basic Books.
Jovanovic, Boyan (1982). 'Inflation and Welfare in the Steady State'. *Journal of Political Economy.* Vol. 90, No. 3, pp. 561–577.
Kahf, Monzer (1978). 'Islamic Economic System: A Review'. Plainsfield, Indiana: *Al-Ittihad.*
Khan, M. Akram (1981). 'Book Review'. *Impact International,* 23 October – 12 November.
Khan, M. Ali (1991). 'Theoretical Studies in Islamic Banking: A Review'. Unpublished paper.
Khan, M. Ali (1992a). Irony in/of Economic Theory. (Mimeo) Paper

REFERENCES

delivered at a Colloquim on Intercultural Comparisons. Johns Hopkins University.

Khan, M. Ali (1992b). Relevance of Functional Analysis to Economic Theory (Mimeo) Working Paper 286, Department of Economics, Johns Hopkins University.

Khan, M. Ali (1991). On the Languages of the Markets. The *Pakistan Development Review*. 30:4(Part I), 503–545.

Khan, M. Ali and Y. Sun (1990). On a Reformulation of Cournot-Nash Equilibria. *Journal of Mathematical Analysis and Application*. 146, 442–460.

Khan, Mahmood Hasan (1982). 'Book Review'. *Hamdard Islamicus*, Vol. 5, No. 2, (Karachi) pp. 91–94.

Khan, Mohsin S., and Abbas Mirakhor (ed.) (1987). *Theoretical Studies in Islamic Banking and Finance*. Houston, Texas: The Institute for Research and Islamic Studies. (Especially Chapter 1 by Mohsin Khan and Abbas Mirakhor, Chapter 3 by Mohsin S. Khan and Chapter 7 by Nadeem-ul-Haq and Abbas Mirakhor).

—— and Abbas Mirakhor (1990). 'Islamic Banking: Experience in the Islamic Republic of Iran and in Pakistan'. *Economic Development and Cultural Change*. Vol. 38, No. 2.

Khan, W. M. (1985). *Towards an Interest-free Islamic Economic System: A Theoretical Analysis of Prohibiting Debt Financing*. Leicester and Islamabad: The Islamic Foundation and the International Association for Islamic Economics.

Koopmans, S. T. C. (1957). *Three Essays on the State of Economic Science*. New York: McGraw-Hill.

Kotlikoff, Laurence J. (1989). Social Security. In John Eatwell, Murray Milgate and Peter Newman (eds.), *Social Economics (The New Palgrave)*. London: Macmillan.

Lakatos, Imre (1970). 'Falsification and Methodology of Scientific Research Programme'. In I. Lakatos and A. Musgrave (eds.), *Criticism and Growth of Knowledge*. Cambridge: Cambridge University Press.

Lindahl, Eric (1960). 'Tax Principles and Tax Policy'. *International Economic Papers*. pp .7–32.

Lindblom, Charles E. (1977). *Politics and Markets: The World's Political-economic Systems*. New York: Basic Books.

Machlup, Fritz (1956). 'Rejoinder to a Reluctant Ultra-empiricist'. *Southern Economic Journal*. Vol. 22, pp. 483–493.

Mandel, Ernest (1990). Karl Marx. In John Eatwell, Murray Milgate and Peter Newman (eds.), *Marxian Economics (The New Palgrave)*. London: Macmillan.

Mangla, I. U. and J. Y. Uppal (1990). Islamic Banking: A Survey of Some Operational Issues. *Research in Financial Services*. Vol. 2. JAI Press, Inc. Pages 179–215.

Marglin, S. A. (1963). 'Social Rate of Discount and the Optimal Rate of Investment'. *The Quarterly Journal of Economics*. Vol. 77, No. 1, pp. 95–111.

Marshall T. N. (1950). *Citizenship and Social Class*. Cambridge: Cambridge University Press.

Marx, K. (1848). *The Manifesto of the Communist Party*. In *Collected Works* VI, Moscow: Progress, 1976.

Marx, Karl (1859). *A Contribution to the Critique of Political Economy*. Moscow: Progress Publishers (1977).

Marx, Karl, and Engels F. (1845–6). *The German Ideology*. London: Lawrence and Wishart, 1940.

Mawdudi, Syed Abul A'la (1976). *Human Rights in Islam*. Leicester: The Islamic Foundation.

Meade, James (1955). *Trade and Welfare*. London: Oxford University Press.

Mishan, E. J. (1967). *The costs of Economic Growth*. London: Staples Press.

Mueller, Dennis (1979). *Public Choice*. Cambridge: Cambridge University Press.

Murphy, J. G. (1970). *The Philosophy of the Right*. London: Macmillan.

Naqvi, Syed Nawab Haider (1971). *Egalitarianism versus Growthmanship*. Karachi: Pakistan Institute of Development Economics.

────── (1977) 'Islamic Economic System: Fundamental Issues'. *Islamic Studies*.

────── (1978). 'Ethical Foundations of Islamic Economics'. *Islamic Studies*.

────── (1981). *Ethics and Economics: An Islamic Synthesis*. Leicester: The Islamic Foundation.

────── (1981a). *Individual Freedom, Social Welfare and Islamic Economic Order*. Islamabad: Pakistan Institute of Development Economics.

────── (1981b). *On Replacing the Institution of Interest in a Dynamic Islamic Economy*. Islamabad: Pakistan Institute of Development Economics.

────── (1982). 'Rejoinder to Volker Nienhaus's Review'. *Orient*. No. 1, pp. 122–124.

────── (1989). 'A Programme for Islamizing Pakistan's Economy'. *PIDE TIDINGS*. Vol. 1, Nos. 1 & 2, pp. 3–9.

────── (1993). *Development Economics: A New Paradigm*. New Delhi: SAGE Publications.

────── and Asghar Qadir (1985). 'Incrementalism and Structural Change: A Technical Note'. *The Pakistan Development Review*. Vol. 24, No. 2, pp. 87–102.

────── and Asghar Qadir (1986). *A Model of a Dynamic Islamic Economy and the Institution of Interest*. Islamabad: Pakistan Institute of Development Economics.

──────, H. U. Beg, Rafiq Ahmed and Mian M. Nazeer (1980). *An Agenda for Islamic Economic Reform*. Islamabad: Pakistan Institute of Development Economics.

──────, H. U. Beg, Rafiq Ahmed and Mian M. Nazeer (1984). *Principles of Islamic Economic Reform*. Islamabad: Pakistan Institute of Development Economics.

Nasr, Seyyed Hossein (1968). *Science and Civilization in Islam*. New York: New American Library.

────── (1968). *Man and Nature*. London: George Allen and Unwin Ltd.

REFERENCES

────── (1979). *Ideals and Realities of Islam*. London: George Allen and Unwin.

────── (1982). 'Book Review'. *Hamdard Islamicus*, Vol. 5, No. 2, pp. 89–91.

────── (1987). 'God', Chapter 16 in Seyyed Hossein Nasr (ed.), *Islamic Spirituality: Foundations*. London: Routledge & Kegan Paul.

Nasr, Seyyed Vali Raza (1987). Towards a Philosophy of Islamic Economics. *The Muslim World*. Vol. LXXVII, No: 3–4. (July–October). pages 175–196.

Nazeer, Mian M. (1982). *The Islamic Economic System: A Few Highlights*. Islamabad: Pakistan Institute of Development Economics.

Nienhaus, Volker (1981). 'Book Review'. *Orient*. Vol. 27, No. 2, pp. 314–316. See also my reply in the same journal. Vol. 23, No. 1, (1982) pp. 122–124.

Novikov, P. S. (1964). *Elements of Mathematical Logic*. London: Addison-Wesley Publishing Co.

Nozick, Robert (1974). *Anarchy, State and Utopia*. New York: Basic Books.

Pickthall, Muhammed Marmaduke (ed.) (1979). *The Meaning of the Glorious Quran*. New York: Asia Book Corp.

Pigou, A. C. (1962). *Economics of Welfare*, 4th Edn. London: English Language Book Society.

Pindyck, Robert S. (1988). 'Risk Aversion and Determinants of Stock Market Behaviour'. *The Review of Economics and Statistics*. Vol. 70, No. 2, pp. 183–190.

Pontryagin, L. S., et al. (1962). *Mathematical Theory of Optimal Processes*. New York: Inter-Science.

Popper, Karl R. (1980). *The Logic of Scientific Discovery*. London: Hutchison. 10th (revised) impression. First published in English in 1959.

Quirk, J., and R. Saposnik (1968). *Introduction to General Equilibrium Theory and Welfare Economics*. New York: McGraw-Hill Book Co. Ltd.

Qutb, Syed (1976). 'An Islamic Approach to Social Justice'. In Khurshid Ahmad (ed.), *Islam: Its Meaning and Message*. London: Islamic Council of Europe.

Rahman, Fazlur (1964). 'Riba and Interest'. *Islamic Studies*. Vol. 3, No. 1.

Rahman, Fazlur (1968). *Islam*. New York: Doubleday.

Ramsey, Frank P. (1928). 'A Mathematical Theory of Saving'. *Economic Journal*. Vol. 38, No. 152, pp. 543–559.

Rawls, John (1971). *A Theory of Justice*. Cambridge, Mass.: Harvard University Press.

────── (1985). 'Justice as Fairness: Politics not Metaphysical'. *Philosophy and Public Affairs*. Vol. 14, No. 3, pp. 223–251.

Robbins, Lionel (1932). *An Essay on the Nature and Significance of Economic Science*. London: Macmillan.

Rodinson, Maxime (1978). *Islam and Capitalism* (English translation). New York: Pantheon Books. (The original French edition appeared in 1966).

Rousseau, J. J. (1968). *The Social Contract* (English translation by Maurice Cranston). Harmondsworth: Penguin Books.

Russell, Bertrand (1964). *Freedom and Organization, 1814–1914*. London: George Allen and Unwin.

—— (1977). *Education and the Social Order.* London: George Allen & Unwin.
Sadr, Mohammad Baqir (1982). *Our Economics* (English translation), Vol. 1, Part 2. Tehran: World Organization for Islamic Services.
Schultz, T. W. (1960). 'Capital Formation by Education'. *Journal of Political Economy.* Vol. 68, No. 6, pp. 571–583.
Schuon, Frithjof (1963). *Understanding Islam.* London: George Allen and Unwin.
—— (1975). *The Transcendent Unity of Religion.* New York: Harper and Row.
—— (1976). *Islam and the Perennial Philosophy.* London: World of Islam Festival Publishing Co. Ltd.
Sen, A. K. (1970). *Collective Choice and Social Welfare.* San Francisco: Holden-Day, Inc.
—— (1983). *Choice, Welfare, and Measurement.* Oxford: Basil Blackwell.
—— (1985). 'Well-being, Agency, and Freedom'. *Journal of Philosophy.*
—— (1987). *On Ethics and Economics.* Oxford: Basil Blackwell.
Shafi, Mufti Mohammad (1968). *Distribution of Wealth in Islam.* (English translation by Muhammad Hasan Askri and Karrar Hussain). Karachi: Ashraf Publications.
Shahrastani, 'Abd al-Karim (1978). *Al-Milal Wa'l Nihal*, Cairo.
Shariati, Ali (1974). *On the Sociology of Islam* (English translation by Hamid Algar). Berkeley, Calif.: Mizan Press.
al-Sibai, Mustafa (n. d.). *Ishtirakiyyat al-Islam* (Islamic Socialism). 3rd edn. Cairo: al-dar al-qawmiyya li-tibaa wa al-nashr. Cited in Rodinson (1979), p. 177.
Siddiqi, Mohammad Nejatullah (1983). *Issues in Islamic Banking.* Leicester: The Islamic Foundation.
—— (1983a). *Banking without Interest.* Leicester: The Islamic Foundation.
Simon, Herbert (1957). *Models of Man.* New York: John Wiley & Sons.
—— (1983). *Reason in Human Affairs.* Oxford: Basil Blackwell.
Smith, Adam (1776). *An Enquiry into the Nature and Causes of the Wealth of Nations.* Edited by Edwin Cannan (1904) London: Methuen.
Stigler, George J. (1981). 'Economics or Ethics?'. In Sterling M. McMurrin (ed.), *The Tanner Lectures on Human Values (Vol. II).* Cambridge: Cambridge University Press.
Sulaiman, Abdul Hamid Abu (1979). 'The Theory of Economics of Islam: The Economics of *Tawhid* and Brotherhood'. In *Contemporary Aspects of Economic and Social Thinking.* Plainsfield, Indiana: M. S. A.
Taleghani, Ayatullah Sayyid Mahmud (1982). *Society and Economics in Islam.* Translated from the Persian by R. Campbell, with annotations and introduction by Hamid Algar. Berkeley, Calif.: Mizan Press.
Thurow, Lester C. (1969). *Poverty and Discrimination.* Washington, D. C.: Brookings Institution.
Tinbergen, Jan (1958). *The Design of Development.* Baltimore: The Johns Hopkins University Press.
Tocqueville, Alexis De (1944). *Democracy in America.* ed Phillips Bradley. 2 Vol. New York: Knopf.

REFERENCES

Toynbee, Arnold (1963). *A Study of History.* (Abridgedment of Volumes I–IV by D. C. Somervell) London: Oxford University Press.

Viner, Jacob (1978). 'Protestantism and the Rise of Capitalism'. *History of Political Economy.* Vol. 10, No. 1. (The article is Chapter 4 of the author's unfinished work, *Religious Thought and Economic Society*).

Watt, W. Montgomery (1948). *Free Will and Pre-Destination in Early Islam.* London: Luzac & Company Ltd.

Weber, Max (1949). *The Methodology of the Social Sciences.* London: Macmillan.

Wensinck, A. J. (1932). *The Muslim Creed.* London: Frank Cass.

Wilson, Rodney (1990). *Islamic Financial Markets.* London and New York: Routledge. Also see the review of the book by Syed Nawab Haider Naqvi, *Journal of Economic Studies.* Vol. 18, No. 1. 1991. pp. 65–67.

Zakaria, Rafiq (1991). *Muhammed and the Quran.* New Delhi: Penguin.

Zamagni, Stephano (1987). Economic Laws. In John Eatwell, Murray Milgate and Peter Newman (eds.), *The Invisible Hand (The New Palgrave).* London: Macmillan.

INDEX

Abduh, Shaykh Mohammad, 35, 36, 164
Abu Dharr, 108, 163
Ahmad, Khurshid, 35, 37, 51, 164, 169
Ahmed, Rafiq, 168
al Ihsan (equilibrium), 25, 27, 36, 60, 61, 104, 157, 158
ad-Adl (social balance), 104
al-Mizan, 36
Al-Sibai, Mustafa, 81, 170
Aleshina, I. V., 70, 164
Ali, Abdullah Yusuf, 117, 164
Ali, Ahmed, 9, 164
Ali, Syed Ameer, 36, 37, 164
alim (a knowledgeable person), 91
Allah, 15, 27, 56, 68, 83, 91, 97, 105, 108, 162
Allama Muhammad Iqbal, 35
allowability constraint, 6, 58, 149
amoral economic theorems, 4
Anwar, Muhammed, 128, 164
Aron, Raymond, 75, 81, 82, 164
Arrow, Kenneth J., 23, 49, 51, 60, 63, 65–7, 70, 106, 115, 164
Aryan, 151
Asaria, Mohammad Iqbal, 165
ascension, 1, 33
Asharite, 35
Atkinson, A. B., 101

Beg, H. U., 168
Bell, Richard, 21, 165
Bentham, 91, 166

Benthamite utilitarianism, 6, 52, 57
Bismark, 108
Blaug, Mark, 22, 23, 165
Bliss, Christopher, 93, 123, 151, 165
Boer, De, 35, 165
Boisard, Marcel A., 21, 35, 68, 81, 165
Briggs, A., 79, 165
Britain, 83
Brumberg, 119
Bulletin, the State Bank of Pakistan, 142, 143

caliphs, 16
capitalism, 2, 3, 5, 7, 71, 72, 75–9, 81–3, 105, 108, 111, 155, 156, 169, 171
Caterphores, George, 35, 165
Central Bank, 116
changeability, 21
Chapra, M. Umer, 128, 129, 165
Christian, 68
Coleman, James S., 97, 165
communist, 3, 72, 81, 82, 168
cultural mores, 2

Deane, Phyllis, 23, 165
Debreu, Gerard, 51, 69, 165
Diamond, P., 70, 165
dichotomy, 1
distributive justice, 57, 61, 62, 72,

INDEX

81, 87–95, 97, 100, 101, 103, 104, 106, 107, 147, 151, 158
Divine approval, 3
Divine Law, 15, 27, 30, 31, 152

Eaton, Charles le Ga, 35, 36, 165
eclectic, 3
economic behaviour, 2, 4, 5, 13, 15, 16, 20, 21, 24, 41, 42, 49, 53, 54, 56, 64, 66, 67, 152, 154, 155, 159
economic growth, 2, 8, 28, 81, 83, 88, 92–5, 103, 104, 106, 107, 115, 149, 158, 159, 168
economic science, 3, 18, 19, 23, 154, 165, 167, 169
Egypt, 35
Engels, F., 82, 168
equilibrium, 6, 25–9, 34, 36, 41, 44–6, 50, 53, 57, 59–64, 67, 68, 79, 80, 83, 87, 89, 94, 95, 101, 102, 107, 108, 114–16, 125, 134, 155, 157, 158, 160, 169
ethico-religious, 5, 50
ethics, 4, 5, 7, 24, 26, 34, 41, 47, 51, 101, 125; framework, 3, 80

fardh (responsibility), 31
Fatima (the Prophet's daughter), 150
fiat, 120, 121
fiqh (Islamic juridical), 154
Fisherian, 112, 118
free will, 6, 25, 26, 29, 31, 34, 41, 44–6, 50, 51, 53, 56, 57, 64, 73, 75, 78, 88, 155, 157, 171
Friedman, Milton, 96, 165

Gamal al-Din al-Afghani, 35
Gemignani, M. C., 118, 165
Germany, 83, 108
gharar (aleatory transactions), 118
Gibb, H. A. R., 9, 15, 35, 165
Gierths, 150
Gough, I., 79, 83, 165
Guillame, Alfred, 102, 166

Hadley, G., 51, 166
Hahn, F. H., 70, 166

Haque, Ziaul, 107, 108, 117, 129, 166
Harrison, Ross, 97, 166
Harsanyi, John C., 19, 20, 49, 52, 166
Hashmi, Alamgir, 22, 166
Hausman, Daniel M., 23, 52, 166
Hegel, 82
Heilbroner, 77, 78
Hollis, Martin, 70, 166
humanistic ethics, 9
Hume, David, 22, 150, 166
Hunt, J. M., 152, 166
Husayn (the Prophet's grandson), 163

ijtihad (legalistic interpretation), 100, 126
India-Pakistan, 35
individual, 1, 3, 7, 10, 18, 22, 25, 27, 30–7, 42, 48, 49, 55–9, 63, 65–8, 70, 72–80, 82, 83, 88–91, 96, 97, 101–3, 105–7, 113–15, 118, 119, 130, 140, 147, 156, 158, 160, 164, 168
individual freedom, 7, 10, 30–2, 55, 56, 72, 73, 75, 76, 78, 79, 83, 88, 89, 96, 106, 140, 147, 156, 158, 168
Ingram, 112, 122
Inshaallah (God willing), 15
Iqbal, Mohammad, 9, 36, 37, 163, 166
Iqbal, Zubair, 136, 151, 166
Iran, 9, 135, 136, 150, 151, 154, 167
Islam, 1–4, 6–9, 13, 14, 20, 22, 24, 26, 28, 30–2, 34–6, 41, 43–50, 52–8, 60, 62, 64, 66, 71–82, 88, 90, 91, 94, 96, 98, 100–6, 108, 112, 114, 118, 124–8, 130, 140, 146, 150, 152–4, 156–66, 168–71
Islam's ethical perceptions, 6, 26
Islam's power, 2
Islamic, 1–10, 13–21, 23–34, 36, 37, 41, 42, 44–69, 71–83, 87–118, 120–31, 134, 136, 139–41, 143–61, 163–71; beliefs, 24; credentials, 8, 153; economic system, 2, 3, 5, 7, 21, 44–7, 71,

INDEX

72, 81, 96, 112, 118, 155, 156, 158, 159, 166–9; economics, 3–6, 8, 10, 13–21, 23, 24, 41, 42, 44, 45, 47–50, 52–4, 58, 60–2, 68, 69, 81, 82, 87, 96, 110, 128, 152–6, 166–9; economy, 2, 7, 13, 18, 24, 47, 50, 53–5, 58, 59, 61, 62, 65–8, 71–3, 75, 76, 78–81, 87, 92–8, 99, 103–7, 110–12, 114, 115, 118, 120, 123, 125–7, 146, 149, 152, 154, 155, 158, 168; ethics, 4, 5, 7, 24, 26, 34, 41, 47, 51, 101, 125, 126, 130, 158; framework, 3, 80; injunctions, 8; philosophy, 1, 105; policy, 3, 8, 103, 111; propositions, 2; religion, 4, 24; society, 14, 16, 24, 27, 45, 53, 56, 58, 59, 65, 73, 78, 92, 93, 95, 98, 115, 139, 147, 149, 152, 158, 159; truths, 8; values, 161; vision, 1, 26, 154
Islamization, 98, 144–51, 160

jabriya, 35
Jencks, Christopher, 151, 166
jihad (a war aginst evil), 36
Jovanovic, Boyan, 119, 166

Kahf, Monzer, 108, 166
Kant, 30, 96
Karbala, 163
kasb (doctrine of acquisition), 35
Keynesian revolution, 23
khalifa (God's vicegerent), 25, 30, 32, 51
Khan, M. Akram, 166
Khan, M. Ali, 3, 18, 23, 69, 118, 166, 167
Khan, Mohsin S., 129, 150, 167
Khan, W. M., 128, 129, 167
khas deposits, 141
khums (a type of tax), 102, 105
Koopmans, S. T. C., 118, 167
Kotlikoff, Laurence J., 108, 167
Kramers, J. H., 35, 165

Lakatos, Imre, 52, 167
Lindahl, Eric, 151, 167
Lindblom, Charles E., 82, 167

Machlup, Fritz, 23, 51, 167
mahana amdani (monthly income), 136
Makka, 36
mal-al-Allah (wealth of God), 108
mal-al-Muslimin (wealth of the Muslims), 108
Mandell, Ernest, 75
Mangla, I. U., 150, 167
Marglin, S. A., 119, 167
Marshall, T. N., 79, 97, 167
Marx, Karl, 9, 74, 75, 82, 147, 167, 168
Marxist economics, 3
Mawdudi, Syed Abul A'la, 36, 168
maximum employment, 88, 95
Meade, James, 107, 168
micro, 6, 23, 51
Mirakhor, Abbas, 129, 136, 150, 166, 167
Mirrlees, J. A., 70, 165
Mishan, E. J., 98, 168
mizan (balance), 25, 34, 36, 170
Modigliani, 119
mono-economists, 18
Mu'awiya, 108
mudaraba (profit-and-loss sharing (PLS), 8, 100, 110, 121
Mueller, Dennis, 49, 168
Muhammad, 35, 98, 164, 170
murabaha (a type of transaction), 128
Murphy, J. G., 96, 168
musharaka (a type of transaction), 128, 141, 144
Muslim, 2–6, 8, 9, 13–28, 36, 41, 42, 44, 45, 50, 51, 53–5, 58, 61, 68, 71, 82, 83, 87, 96, 101, 102, 104, 105, 109, 114, 120, 126, 128, 129, 139, 146, 148, 149, 152–5, 157–61, 163, 165, 166, 169, 171; behaviour, 4; economists, 2, 3, 17, 20, 42, 51, 61, 114, 120, 129, 149, 160; philosophers, 2; society, 2, 4–6, 9, 13, 14, 16, 17, 19, 20, 24, 27, 28, 36, 44, 50, 53, 54, 58, 68, 87, 96, 102, 104, 139, 146, 149, 152–5, 160; theologians, 8

174

INDEX

mustadafin (oppressed class), 74
mustakbarin (oppressor class), 74

Naqvi, Syed Nawab Haider, 5, 10, 23, 34, 36, 37, 51, 52, 60
Nasr, Seyyed Vali Raza, 36, 68, 169
Nasr, Seyyed Hossein, 9, 36, 68, 94, 163, 165, 168, 169
National Investment Trust (NIT), 141
Nazeer, Mian M., 68, 168, 169
neoclassical, 3, 6, 13, 14, 18, 20, 21, 23, 52, 55, 57–62
neoclassical economics, 3, 13, 18, 20, 23, 55, 57, 58, 60–2
Nienhaus, Volker, 169
non-consequentialism, 6, 57
Novikov, P. S., 51, 169
Nozick, Robert, 48, 51, 52, 57, 96, 108, 169

operative axioms, 4

Pakistan, 9, 35, 108, 117, 129, 133–6, 141–4, 150, 154
Pakistan Economic Survey, 142, 150
Pareto-optimality, 3, 6, 48, 49, 60–2, 66–9, 155
philosophers, 2; society, 2, 4–6, 9, 13, 14, 16, 17, 19, 20, 24
Pickthall, Muhammed Marmaduke, 9, 169
Pigou, A. C., 119, 169
policy instruments, 3, 7, 8, 81, 99, 100, 107, 110, 111, 117
political totalitarianism, 3
Pontryagin, L. S., 118, 169
Popper, Karl R., 21, 22, 44, 51, 150, 153, 162, 169
positivistic, 3, 75
Prisoner's Dilemma Case, 48
Property Rights, 4, 34, 47, 48, 65, 69, 76, 78, 82, 100–3
Prophet, 16, 41, 128, 139, 140, 150, 163
Pythagorean, 157

qadariya, 35

Qadir, Asghar, 63, 107, 118, 119, 127, 129, 151, 168
qard al-Hasana (sort-term interest-free loans), 136
qist (equity), 25, 89
Quirk, J., 69, 169
Quraish, 128
Quran, 6, 8, 9, 21, 25, 27, 28, 30, 33, 34, 36, 41, 43, 47
Qutb, Syed, 36, 52, 169

Rahman, Fazlur, 36, 107, 117, 169
Ramsey, Frank P., 119, 169
rational behaviour, 3, 20, 55–8, 67
Rawls, John, 31, 51, 52, 56, 65, 69, 151, 169
relativity, 5, 9, 21, 36, 37, 73, 80, 154
responsibility, 6, 7, 24–6, 30–4, 37, 41, 44–6, 48, 50, 53, 56, 57, 65, 72–4, 78–80, 83, 88, 95, 96, 101, 155–8, 160
riba (usury), 8, 99, 100, 110–12, 117, 118, 120, 128, 129, 149, 166, 169
Ricardian economics, 22
Robbins, Lionel, 20, 21, 23, 48, 49, 52, 69, 169
Rodinson, Maxime, 76, 82, 169, 170
Rousseau, J. J., 96, 169
Russell, Bertrand, 70, 83, 98, 169

sadaqa (charity, altruistic behaviour), 128
Sadr, Mohammad Baqir, 2, 19, 36, 37, 52, 65, 82, 107, 151, 170
sanad (authority), 153
Saposnik, R., 69, 169
Sayyid Ahmed Khan, 35
Sayyid Ameer Ali, 35
Schultz, T. W., 152, 170
Schuon, Frithjof, 35–7, 170
secular, 1, 18, 22, 113, 157
Sen, A. K., 52, 60, 68–70, 170
Shafi, Mufti Mohammad, 83, 108, 170
Shahrastani, 'Abd al-Karim, 35, 170

INDEX

Shariati, Ali, 170
Siddiqi, Mohammad Nejatullah, 121, 126, 128, 129, 170
Simon, Herbert, 48, 70, 170
slavery, 9, 31, 33, 140, 157
Smith, Adam, 57, 68, 170
social justice, 3, 15, 25, 45, 90, 95–7, 102, 132, 161, 169
socialism, 2, 5, 7, 21, 71–5, 78, 79, 81, 83, 105, 155, 156, 170
socialist, 3, 65, 72, 73
socio-economic, 1, 8, 26, 46, 76, 108, 110, 145, 152, 158
Soviet Union, 3
spherical geometry, 9
spiritual, 1, 9, 25, 33, 46, 81, 82, 91, 93, 148, 156, 157, 159
Stigler, George J., 69, 82, 170
Sulaiman, Abdul Hamid Abu, 52, 170
sunnah, 6, 8, 41, 43, 47, 54
Syndicalism, 83

Taleghani, Ayatullah Sayyid Mahmud, 52, 65, 82, 97, 107–9
tawhid (unity), 26, 164, 170
theomorphic, 1, 25, 30, 160
Thurow, Lester C., 151, 170
Tinbergen, Jan, 107, 170
Tocqueville, Alexis de, 151, 170
Toynbee, Arnold, 163, 171
trusteeship, 27, 66, 80, 82, 90
Turkey, 35

Ulama, 150
ultra-empiricists, 18, 23, 53
United States, 129, 134, 151
unity, 6, 26–9, 34, 36, 41, 44–6, 50, 53, 94, 155, 159, 163, 164, 170
universal education, 8, 88, 91, 95, 146, 148, 158
Uppal, J. Y., 150, 167
ushr (a kind of tax), 102, 105
utility-maximizing calculus, 6

value-free economics, 4
Viner, Jacob, 77, 171

Weber, Max, 19, 44, 171
welfare state, 2, 5, 7, 71, 72, 81, 83, 109, 156, 165
weltanschauung, 74
Wensinck, A. J., 35, 171
Wilson, Rodney, 150, 151, 171
Wittgenstein, Ludwig, 22

Yazid, 163

Zaid, 150
Zakaria, Rafiq, 150, 171
zakat (a kind of tax), 22, 102, 105, 136, 159
Zamagni, Stephano, 20, 171
Zia Grkalp, 35
zulm (social disequilibrium), 28, 29, 45, 60, 61, 157, 158